THE NATIVE AMERICANS

THE NATIVE AMERICANS

Other books in this series include:

The History of Weapons and Warfare

The Native Americans

Don Nardo

LUCENT
BOOKS®

THOMSON
★
™
GALE

San Diego • Detroit • New York • San Francisco • Cleveland • New Haven, Conn. • Waterville, Maine • London • Munich

Cover caption: A Florida tribe of Native Americans attacks a village with fire arrows.

LIBRARY OF CONGRESS CATALOGING-IN-PUBLICATION DATA

Nardo, Don, 1947–
  The Native Americans / by Don Nardo.
p. cm. — (The history of weapons and warfare)
Summary: Discusses the weapons used by Native Americans and their different
means of warfare.
Includes bibliographical references and index.
  ISBN 1-59018-070-4 (hardback : alk. paper)
  1. Indians of North America—Warfare. 2. Military art and sciences—History—
19th century. 3. Military history, Modern—19th century. 4. Military weapons—
History—19th century.] I. Title. II. Series.
  E98.W2 N37 2003
  355'.0089'97—dc21
                                                          2002008589

Printed in the United States of America

Contents

Foreword

The earliest battle about which any detailed information has survived took place in 1274 B.C. at Kadesh, in Syria, when the armies of the Egyptian and Hittite empires clashed. For this reason, modern historians devote a good deal of attention to Kadesh. Yet they know that this battle and the war of which it was a part were not the first fought by the Egyptians and their neighbors. Many other earlier conflicts are mentioned in ancient inscriptions found throughout the Near East and other regions, as from the dawn of recorded history city-states fought one another for political or economic dominance.

Moreover, it is likely that warfare long predated city-states and written records. Some scholars go so far as to suggest that the Cro-Magnons, the direct ancestors of modern humans, wiped out another early human group—the Neanderthals—in a prolonged and fateful conflict in the dim past. Even if this did not happen, it is likely that even the earliest humans engaged in conflicts and battles over territory and other factors. "Warfare is almost as old as man himself," writes renowned military historian John Keegan, "and reaches into the most secret places of the human heart, places where self dissolves rational purpose, where pride reigns, where emotion is paramount, where instinct is king."

Even after humans became "civilized," with cities, writing, and organized religion, the necessity of war was widely accepted. Most people saw it as the most natural means of defending territory, maintaining security, or settling disputes. A character in a dialogue by the fourth-century B.C. Greek thinker Plato declares:

> All men are always at war with one another. . . . For what men in general term peace is only a name; in reality, every city is in a natural state of war with every other, not indeed proclaimed by heralds, but everlasting. . . . No possessions or institutions are of any value to him who is defeated in battle; for all the good things of the conquered pass into the hands of the conquerors.

Considering the thousands of conflicts that have raged across the world since Plato's time, it would seem that war is an inevitable part of the human condition.

War not only remains an ever-present reality, it has also had undeniably crucial and far-reaching effects on human society and its development. As Keegan puts it, "History lessons remind us that the states in which we live . . . have come to us through conflict, often of the most bloodthirsty sort." Indeed, the world's first and oldest nation-state,

Egypt, was born out of a war between the two kingdoms that originally occupied the area; the modern nations of Europe rose from the wreckage of the sweeping barbarian invasions that destroyed the Roman Empire; and the United States was established by a bloody revolution between British colonists and their mother country.

Victory in these and other wars resulted from varying factors. Sometimes the side that possessed overwhelming numbers or the most persistence won; other times superior generalship and strategy played key roles. In many cases, the side with the most advanced and deadly weapons was victorious. In fact, the invention of increasingly lethal and devastating tools of war has largely driven the evolution of warfare, stimulating the development of new counter-weapons, strategies, and battlefield tactics. Among the major advances in ancient times were the composite bow, the war chariot, and the stone castle. Another was the Greek phalanx, a mass of close-packed spearman marching forward as a unit, devastating all before it. In medieval times, the stirrup made it easier for a rider to stay on his horse, increasing the effectiveness of cavalry charges. And a progression of late medieval and modern weapons—including cannons, handguns, rifles, submarines, airplanes, missiles, and the atomic bomb—made warfare deadlier than ever.

Each such technical advance made war more devastating and therefore more feared. And to some degree, people are drawn to and fascinated by what they fear, which accounts for the high level of interest in studies of warfare and the weapons used to wage it. Military historian John Hackett writes:

An inevitable result of the convergence of two tendencies, fear of war and interest in the past, has seen a thirst for more information about the making of war in earlier times, not only in terms of tools, techniques, and methods used in warfare, but also of the people by whom wars are and have been fought and how men have set about the business of preparing for and fighting them.

These themes—the evolution of warfare and weapons and how it has affected various human societies—lie at the core of the books in Lucent's History of Weapons and Warfare series. Each book examines the warfare of a pivotal people or era in detail, exploring the beliefs about and motivations for war at the time, as well as specifics about weapons, strategies, battle formations, infantry, cavalry, sieges, naval tactics, and the lives and experiences of both military leaders and ordinary soldiers. Where possible, descriptions of actual campaigns and battles are provided to illustrate how these various factors came together and decided the fate of city, a nation, or a people. Frequent quotations by contemporary participants or observers, as well as by noted modern military historians, add depth and authenticity. Each volume features an extensive annotated bibliography to guide those readers interested in further research to the most important and comprehensive works on warfare in the period in question. The series provides students and general readers with a useful means of understanding what is regrettably one of the driving forces of human history—violent human conflict.

Two Very Different Concepts of Warfare

The history of the weapons and warfare of the Native Americans whom whites of European origin encountered in the lands now encompassing the United States has two quite distinct dimensions. The first is the use of weapons and war tactics by the native tribes against one another. Intertribal warfare had been a fact of life in North America long before the arrival of white explorers and settlers. And the Indians had developed set methods, styles, and rituals of fighting. Wars were almost always localized, small-scale, and of short duration, which usually predetermined that one's enemy would survive a conflict intact. As Cherokee historian Tom Holm, of the University of Arizona, puts it,

> In general, tribes raided or engaged in pitched battles to obtain material goods, take revenge on traditional enemies for the killing of relatives, seize captives, or vent aggression. Although a few groups, like the . . . Iroquois, were able to assemble large

numbers of warriors into very real armies, territorial conquests and instances of mass slaughter on the scale of those habitually carried out by the Assyrians, Greeks, Romans, Huns, Ottomans, and Spanish did not occur in aboriginal America. . . . And the Iroquois appear to have been much more concerned with adopting captives taken on raids than on the acquisition of territory and the destruction of entire societies.[1]

In contrast, the whites brought with them markedly different concepts and methods of warfare. Major colonization of North America began in the wake of the Thirty Years' War (1618–1648), in which most of the great powers of Europe battled one another for dominance. Driven by extreme religious hatred and rivalry, the participants often resorted to savage "search and destroy" tactics and various atrocities. It is estimated that in some areas of Europe civilian casualties exceeded 50 percent, an unprecedented slaughter. What is more, European settlers brought such methods with them across the Atlantic. In 1637, during one of the first wars between Indians and whites, a group of Connecticut troops and their Indian allies surrounded a Pequot Indian village. After capturing the village, the whites burned it to the ground and murdered all the inhabitants, including women and children; shocked, the Indian allies departed, refusing to participate in the butchery.

This does not mean that Indians never conducted massacres of their own. On occasion they did so, but these incidents were most often the result of frustration, desperation, and revenge precipitated by white aggression and

land theft. The whites not only killed many Indians but also cheated them out of their lands or simply removed them and forced them to relocate in strange lands farther west. The policy of Indian removal and relocation adopted by the U.S. government in the nineteenth century was based on the supposition that Indians could simply pick up and move practically anywhere and find some way to live off the land. But for most Indians, the reality of removal was quite different. Forcing thousands of people to abandon their ancestral homes and move to distant, unfamiliar territories caused untold misery and the destruction of entire ways of life. It also ensured that those Indians who had been defeated

The early European settlers of North America often employed ruthless methods of warfare. Here, Connecticut troops attack an Indian village during the Pequot War.

would stay defeated. Historian Dale Van Every provides this summary of the policy's terrible impact:

> In the long record of man's inhumanity, exile has wrung moans of anguish from many different peoples. Upon no people could it ever have fallen with a more shattering impact than upon the eastern Indians. The Indian was peculiarly susceptible to every sensory attribute of every natural feature of his surroundings. . . . He knew every marsh, glade, hilltop, rock, spring, creek as only the hunter can know them. . . . He felt himself as much a part of [the land] as the rocks and trees, the animals and birds. His homeland was holy ground, sanctified for him as the resting place of the bones of his ancestors and the natural shrine of his religion. He conceived its waterfalls and ridges, its

A drawing shows part of the wide array of muskets, rifles, and other weapons used against Indians by white settlers in the 1600s and 1700s.

clouds and mists, its glens and meadows, to be inhabited by the myriad [large number] of spirits with whom he held daily communion. It was from this rain-washed land of forests, streams, and lakes, to which he was held by the traditions of his forbears . . . that he was to be driven to the arid, treeless plains of the far west, a desolate region then universally known as the Great American Desert. [2]

As a weapon, this cruel policy of removal and relocation was perfectly consistent with the concept of total war that the whites were accustomed to, but the Indians found it inexplicable and barbaric.

The whites also brought with them advanced technology and more lethal standard weaponry than that possessed by Native Americans. These included refined metals for knives, swords, and hatchets, as well as gunpowder and firearms. Through trade, capture, and other means, some Indians acquired these weapons, and over time they spread across the continent to other tribes. Yet the Indians lacked the industrial base to produce such items in large quantities, and they had no way of making gunpowder. As a result, the Indians remained literally outgunned throughout the eighteenth and nineteenth centuries, the crucial period in which they fought for survival against white civilization.

Indeed, these factors—the differing concepts of warfare, the institutionalized removal of peoples from their lands, and the superior weaponry of the whites—proved devastating in the long run. They ensured that the struggles between whites and Indians for control of the continent would be different in tone and outcome than the age-old intertribal contests. Before the arrival of the whites, warfare had been an accepted part of life among most Native American tribes. Yet it had been largely nonlethal and had produced little long-term impact. However, after the coming of the whites—and their superior weapons—the impact was nothing less than the destruction of traditional Indian society in North America.

CHAPTER ONE

Precontact Offensive Weapons

A propensity for making war was one cultural factor that nearly all Native Americans had in common, despite the many differences among the hundreds of tribes inhabiting the United States. Most tribes spoke different languages and viewed themselves as separate nations with distinct cultural identities and local traditions, habits, and values. This reality belied the common white view that all Indians belonged to one more or less monolithic group with a single set of ideas and values. Still, despite the considerable diversity, most of the tribes, especially in the East and Midwest, shared certain basic characteristics. "Whatever their environment," scholars Robert Utley and Wilcomb Washburn point out,

> they lived close to it, finely tuned to its vagaries, able to exploit such food and other resources as it contained, adept at making favorable use of its features, however harsh. They worshiped deities and performed sacred rituals that related primarily to na-

ture. They governed themselves by highly democratic political systems in which leaders carried out the will of the people. They cherished the freedom, independence, and dignity of the individual, the family, and the group.

Perhaps most important, Utley and Washburn emphasize, "With some notable exceptions," these tribes "exalted war and bestowed great prestige on the successful warrior."[3]

To be successful, a warrior needed weapons that were both effective and reliable. Moreover, in the precontact period—that is, before the coming of the whites and their advanced technology and weaponry—Indian weapons had to be made almost entirely by hand and of largely unprocessed natural materials. This presented a considerable challenge. Native Americans had no industrial capacity and were still in a stage of technological development that historians and anthropologists call the Neolithic

Age, or Late Stone Age. Nevertheless, Indians across the continent met the challenge. Using stone, wood, and some unsmelted metals, they fashioned many highly effective striking, cutting, and piercing weapons.

Striking Weapons

Perhaps the oldest striking weapons wielded by Native Americans (as well as by people in cultures worldwide) were simple clubs. An early type of club was monolithic, meaning that both the handle and head were made from a single piece of stone, usually flint or jasper. Some examples had a rounded head, like that of a medieval European mace, while others had a head shaped like an ax blade; the latter usually tapered to an edge so sharp that the weapon could decapitate an opponent in a single stroke. Such weapons

reached their most widespread development and use in the southeastern United States in an arc stretching from Florida to southern Ohio.

More advanced and difficult to make, as well as more widely distributed, was a club with a wooden handle and stone head. According to Colin F. Taylor, an authority on Native American weapons,

The stone head was attached to the handle by shaving thin the upper end of the wooden shaft and then bending it around the groove which had been made in the stone; the pared wood was then lashed into place with rawhide thongs. Alternatively, a broad band of rawhide secured the head to the shaft, which

Native American Tribes

The Great Plains
1 Seneca
2 Cayuga
3 Onondaga
4 Oneida
5 Mohawk

Warriors of two Great Lakes tribes fight one another with clubs and other traditional weapons.

might be inserted into a hole drilled in the stone. The rawhide was generally softened by first soaking it in water and then tightly bound; when it dried, the subsequent shrinkage held the head securely in place.[4]

In an alternative version of the stone-headed club, the stone head was not attached directly and rigidly to the handle. Instead, the weapon maker encased the head in rawhide or heavy buckskin and sewed the bottom edge of material around the wooden handle. That left the head in a loose, free-moving state within the material, imparting a small whiplash effect when the user swung the weapon. Both kinds of clubs were often colorfully decorated with beads, porcupine quills, rawhide strips, carved animals, and so forth.

Still another kind of club common to many North American tribes was made entirely of wood or animal bone or a combination of the two. The so-called ball-headed club, which achieved wide distribution, particularly in the Southwest and Northwest, was carved from a single piece of wood.

Cruder versions had a simple, straight handle; more elaborate ones had slightly curved handles with finely carved grips for the palm and/or fingers. Such clubs could be used either in a traditional overhand stroke to crush a skull or arm or in an upward stroke to shatter an opponent's jaw. (Early English colonists in Virginia called ball-headed clubs tomahawks. But the more common and familiar use of that term came later, in reference to hatchets with metal blades, mostly manufactured by whites but used by both Indians and whites.)

Cutting Weapons

At least as old as clubs were Native American stone-cutting edges that could be used as tools, utensils, or weapons. The simplest variety, distributed throughout North America, was a chisel-shaped blade made from a thin piece of jasper, flint, chert, agate, or basanite. As early as 12,000 B.C., such blades were in use as tools that could scrape, saw, cut holes, or carve. As weapons, they could maim or kill. The most primitive kind of blade was held in the palm of the hand, backed by some padding made of rawhide or another pliable material. More advanced versions were attached to handles made of wood, bone, or horn.

Knives constructed with such stone blades were highly effective weapons, in large part because the edges of the blades were extremely sharp. The sharp edges were accomplished by chipping and beveling the relatively soft stone in a process called flaking. According to Taylor,

The natural edges or forms of the stone were modified by fracturing with a specially made flaking tool. The "flaker," as it was commonly called, had a blade generally of antler [deer or elk horn], ivory, or hard bone,

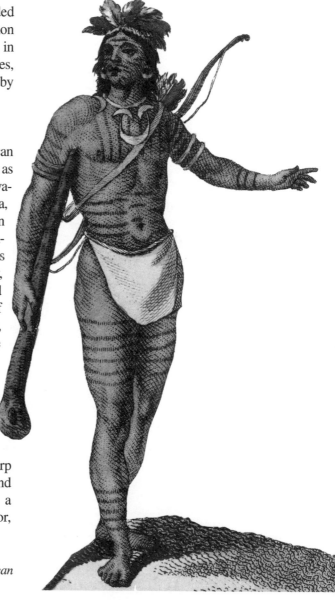

An early Indian warrior native to the Caribbean region carries a ball-headed club.

set in a wooden handle. This was applied to the stone edge and, with a quick movement (at the same time exerting a strong pressure), a flake of the stone was forced off. A skilled individual worked rapidly, moving along the outline of the blade, producing a razor-sharp, although fragile, cutting edge.[5]

A later advancement in Native American blade making occurred shortly before the Europeans established their first colonies in North America. By the late 1500s, and probably considerably earlier, the tribes of the Great Lakes, Mississippi River, and the Northwest coastal regions were fashioning copper knife blades for tools and weapons. This was not smelted, refined copper that had been used for millennia in the Near East and Europe; instead, the copper was in the form of natural nuggets that had been torn loose from copper-bearing rocks by the movement of glaciers during the last ice age. The Indians collected the nuggets and used stone hammers to flatten them into usable blades.

Copper-bladed weapons had some advantages over stone ones. First, the metal blades could more easily be made long and narrow if a longer knife was desired. They could also be given double edges, which made them more effective for both slashing and stabbing. However, pure copper is a fairly soft metal, and a few strong blows against a hard surface will blunt the edge. This limited the value of such weapons in combat situations. But some tribes apparently regarded copper as a special material with magical properties, so copper weapons were often used for ceremonial purposes.

Piercing Weapons

Another weapon that utilized a stone or natural copper blade was the spear, used in both

PRECONTACT TOOLS AND WEAPONS STILL USED

Even after Native American tribes acquired white-made processed metals, they did not completely abandon their traditional tools and weapons of stone, wood, and bone, as explained here by Paul Carlson from his book The Plains Indians.

The bow and arrow remained the preferred weapon. Men often used knives for hand-to-hand combat and the lance continued to be used long after the appearance of firearms. War clubs with stone heads—some spherical, some pointed at both ends, and some ax-shaped—held in place by shrunken rawhide and attached to a wooden handle remained common well after white contact. Men continued to smooth arrow shafts between two grooved stones. Even as they acquired iron implements, they still fashioned some arrow points and knives of bone, stone, and horn. Until recent years women preferred to pound chokecherries and other berries on a flat stone with a grooved-stone hammer. Skin dressers used several tools of bone, horn, and antler, and bone awls served to punch holes for sewing. Nonetheless, in their dynamic material cultures ancient implements tended to give way to modern ones, and thus sometimes scholars are hard pressed to identify all the precontact tools, utensils, and implements.

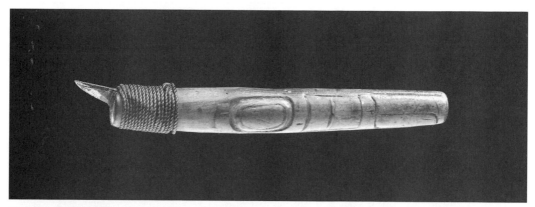

This wooden knife handle features carved designs. Early Native American knives had blades made of stone or hammered copper.

hunting and warfare. The difference between the knife and spear was that the latter was a piercing weapon. A spear could be used in hand-to-hand combat, in which case the user jabbed it overhand at an opponent, similar to the way ancient Greek soldiers jabbed their spears at their enemies. More often, however, the spear was thrown, hurled, or propelled from a spot some distance from the target. Spears came in numerous sizes; whites often referred to the shorter, thinner varieties as "darts."

Only rarely did Native Americans hurl a spear or dart with the hand alone. They preferred instead to propel the weapon with devices that imparted more force to the throw. Some of the tribes along the California coast, for example, among them the Miwok and Pomo, used a rawhide sling to propel the spear. In the southeastern United States, tribes such as the Seminole, Choctaw, and Cherokee developed a blow tube (or blowgun); the user placed a dart in a hollow piece of sugar cane and forced the projectile out by blowing into the back end of the tube. The Spanish explorer Ponce de León was reportedly slain in Florida by a dart from a native blow tube.

Much more common and widely distributed was the atlatl, a Stone Age weapon that long predated the bow and was used at one time or another by hunter-gatherers across the globe. (Atlatl was the name given to the weapon by the Aztec Indians of central and southern Mexico. U.S. tribes had their own various names for it, but modern scholars came to apply the Aztec term to all versions.) The atlatl was a throwing stick. Usually about eighteen inches long, it consisted of a wooden handle attached to a wooden socket or groove. The back end of the spear or dart was inserted into the socket, and the user unleashed the projectile by flipping the stick in a forceful overhand motion. In a sense, the atlatl became a fourth joint in the thrower's arm (the other three being the shoulder, elbow, and wrist), which imparted to the spear considerably more forward momentum than was possible with the arm alone. Another advantage was that the weapon could be discharged using one hand; thus, a warrior could use an atlatl with one arm while rowing a canoe or carrying a fallen comrade with the other.

AN EXTREMELY ANCIENT WEAPON

Grant Keddie, curator of the Royal British Columbia Museum, gives this brief history of the atlatl (excerpted from his article "The Atlatl Weapon"), one of the world's most ancient weapons.

The oldest atlatls in the world date back over 25,000 years in Northwest Africa. The late Upper Paleolithic Magdalenian peoples of Europe made beautifully carved specimens from antler and bone 17,000 years ago. Immigrants from Siberia likely brought the atlatl to North America, where it was used to hunt large animals by at least 10,000–12,000 years ago. Atlatl spears were likely tipped with the large flaked stone points that archaeologists find associated with remains of now-extinct mammoth and bison, as well as other large game animals. In more recent times we know the atlatl was also used for hunting sea mammals, birds, and fish. The Inuit and Aleut of the Arctic, the Tlingit peoples of the southern coast of Alaska and northern coast of British Columbia, and some peoples of southeastern United States, Mexico and northern South America, still used the atlatl when Europeans first arrived. However, in most regions of the New World, the bow and arrow replaced the atlatl. Archaeologists believe that the trend toward small stone projectile points (tips for arrows or spears), and the shift from making these points with tapered bases, as opposed to thinner-necked notched bases, is evidence for the replacement of the atlatl by the bow and arrow. This change in point size and style occurred most typically around 1,350 years ago, but some researchers argue that the bow and arrow was introduced earlier in some areas of North America.

A rare golden atlatl rests in a museum in Colombia. The atlatl was still in use in parts of the Americas when the first whites appeared.

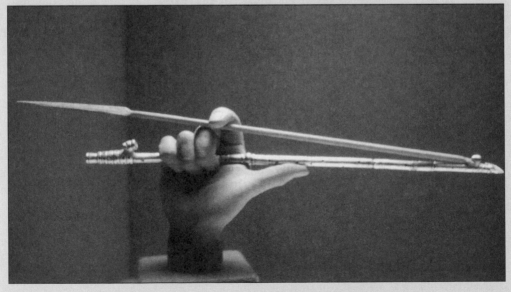

The atlatl was an extremely lethal weapon in the hands of a trained individual. And many Native Americans practiced with it religiously in both peacetime and wartime from an early age. In the 1540s, a member of the expedition of Spaniard Hernando De Soto, the first European to see the Mississippi River, witnessed the use of the atlatl firsthand:

One soldier was wounded with . . . a dart . . . [which] is thrown with a wooden strip [the atlatl]. . . . Our Spaniards had never seen this weapon before that day in any part of Florida through which they had traveled. . . . The strip is of wood two-thirds of a yard in length, and is capable of sending a dart with such great force that it has been seen to pass completely through a man armed with a coat of mail [armor made of metal scales sewn or glued to a heavy jacket]. In Peru, the Spaniards feared this weapon more than any others the Indian possessed, for the arrows there were not so fierce as those of Florida.[6]

A weapon related to the spear was the lance, a longer piercing weapon wielded by a warrior on horseback. Although the horse was introduced to the Indians by the whites (in the early 1600s), the lance can be considered a precontact weapon because it was essentially an adaptation of the spears that had been in use in North America for dozens of centuries. Use of the lance was most common among the horse cultures of the southern plains and Southwest. One southwestern tribe, the Apache, became unusually adept

with the weapon, as recalled by a contemporary observer:

They charge with both hands [holding lances] over their heads, managing their horses principally with their knees. With this weapon they are considered an overmatch for the Spanish dragoons [horsemen] single handed.[7]

The Bow and Arrow

Of all the Native American piercing weapons, the arrow, shot from a bow, was the most common and widely distributed. Virtually every tribe on the continent used the weapon. Experts are unsure exactly when the Indians began using the bow and arrow. But recent scholarship suggests that bows did not reach North America until rather late, several thousand years after the atlatl. In his noted study of Indian bows, scholar Reginald Laubin writes,

There seems to be no evidence of it [the bow] in the earliest cliff dwellings [of the southwestern United States], although it does show up in later ones. It would seem to be of Asiatic origin but was brought over in later migrations [circa 2000 to 1000 B.C.], rather than in the early ones [circa 13,000 to 12,000 B.C.].[8]

The most common variety of Indian bow was the simple or self bow, made of a single piece of bendable, elastic wood. Ash, hickory, and black locust were perhaps the most frequently used wood types. On average, self bows were about five and a half to six feet long. Another kind of bow was the sinew-lined or reinforced bow, so named because the wooden stave had a backing of animal sinew (tendon) to give it more flexibility and power. Most reinforced bows averaged three and a half to four feet in length. They were usually made of wood from ash, cedar, juniper, and wild plum, but many other varieties of tree were also employed. Bowstrings were fashioned from single or double strands of sinew that were knotted around notches carved into the ends of the bow.

Still another kind of bow was constructed from the horns of elk or mountain sheep. The advantage of the horn bow was that horn was tougher than wood and could withstand more compression. Extra layers of sinew were added to the horn, generating more power when the bowman released an arrow. Alfred Miller, a white traveler who witnessed Shoshone warriors using horn bows in 1834, later wrote, "With an elk-horn bow, they sometimes drive an arrow completely through a buffalo."[9]

As for the arrows, precontact versions had heads (or points) made of flint and other

Plains Indians use horn bows to hunt buffalo. This type of bow could withstand more compression and was therefore more powerful than an ordinary bow.

A WARRIOR'S ACCESSORIES

In this excerpt from his informative book Native American Weapons, *scholar Colin Taylor describes some common Indian quivers (arrow holders) and bow cases.*

The style of quiver and bow-case varied greatly from one region to the next. Not only did it depend on the size of the bow and arrows but also on materials readily available. Sealskin was used in the Arctic by such groups as the Central Eskimo; on the West Coast, some quivers were cedar wood whilst various animal skins and pelts were used by the Plateau, Plains, and Woodland tribes and also to a lesser extent by those groups in the southwest, who sometimes also used soft basketry. Styles varied considerably, but the most common was a combined bow-case and separate arrow-case which were laced together and which generally had a strap which went over the shoulder. Some bow-case–quiver combinations were particularly elaborate, such as the elegant and richly decorated ones made from three otterskins with two heavily beaded flaps attached—one at the mouth of the bow-case, the other on the arrow-case. Such magnificent accoutrements [accessories] have been firmly associated with both the Plateau and Plains tribes, particularly the Nez Perce and Crow.

types of stone, as well as horn, bone, wood, seashell, and unprocessed copper. The most common shape for an arrowhead was the triangle. The arrow maker attached the head to the shaft by inserting it in a notch in the shaft's end and lashing it with strips of sinew. There was much more, however, to the arrow-making process, which was both a skill and an art. As Texas Tech University scholar Paul Carlson explains,

Good arrows were not easy to make. Because a crooked arrow or one with improperly placed guide feathers [to make the arrow fly straight] proved worthless, the men took great care in making arrows. They used wood of the gooseberry, juneberry, chokeberry, ash, birch, cane, dogwood, currant, willow, and wild cherry saplings. Lakota [Sioux] men preferred gooseberry, with cherry and juneberry as second choices; Blackfeet men used shoots of the serviceberry, a straight, very heavy, and tough wood; Comanche men preferred young dogwood, with mature ash as a secondary choice. The men cut the shafts to the desired length and shape, tied them in a bunch, and to season them hung them near a fire for about ten days. Then, in a tedious process the arrow-makers straightened the shafts. Over a period of several days, they used their teeth, grease, fire, and a special arrow straightener—a bone or horn with a hole slightly larger than the shaft through which they passed the arrow back and forth—to make the arrow perfectly round. They scraped it to proper size and taper. Most of the better arrows they grooved from the end of the feathers to the head of the arrow point. Next, they polished and painted the shaft.

Finally, they attached the feathers—owl, turkey, or buzzard feathers preferred—with glue and fixed the point.[10]

The arrow-making process, along with the production of other kinds of weapons, clearly illustrates that, despite their lack of sophisticated technology, Native Americans were far from primitive. Their artisans displayed a high level of skill and ingenuity well before contact with white civilization and its tools and weapons.

CHAPTER TWO

Weapons Borrowed from the Whites

From the seventeenth to nineteenth centuries, Native American weapons, which had remained more or less static for many centuries, underwent a sort of revolution. The main cause was the introduction of new and more advanced technology by white European settlers, trappers, traders, and soldiers. The whites knew how to smelt and process metals. And with steel blades, the Indians' knives, spear points, and hatchets became much more efficient and lethal. Even more deadly were the firearms wielded by white settlers and soldiers. It did not take long for these advanced weapons to spread across the continent. In fact, it was not unusual for a tribe to have its way of life, including its methods of making war, transformed long before its members had ever laid eyes on a white person.

Metal-Bladed Hatchets

With a few exceptions, Native Americans usually acquired pieces of metal that had already been refined rather than processing the metals themselves. Over time, some In-

dians became blacksmiths with the skills to forge various kinds of blades. But these artisans were almost always members of tribes that had had long periods of contact with white settlements or that had adopted white ways in an attempt to survive in a rapidly changing world. For the most part, Native Americans in frontier areas continued to lack any meaningful industrial capacity. So, most Indians got the processed metals they needed through trade with whites.

Indeed, white traders recognized early on that the local natives' lack of refined metals for bladed weapons created an important potential market. In exchange for animal hides and pelts, whites at first traded processed metals, which the Indians eagerly hammered into usable blades. Soon, white manufacturers went a step further and began making ready-made knives, hatchets, and other bladed weapons. The volume of trade in such weapons, especially hatchets, became enormous. One English merchant, Sir William Johnson, estimated that he sold about ten thousand hatchets to Indians in

KNIVES WITH SPIRITUAL POWERS?

Many Indians believed that their knives, as well as other weapons, could possess potent spiritual powers. In this excerpt from his book about Native American weapons, scholar Colin Taylor describes the powers and strict rituals associated with the so-called Bear Bundle of the Blackfeet, a Plains tribe.

The chief object in the Bear Bundle was a large dagger-like knife, to the handle of which was attached the jaws of a bear. Although the power of such a knife was considered to be very great . . . few individuals owned these bundles. One reason given was the brutality of the transfer ritual. Thus, the recipient was required to catch the knife thrown violently at him and also to lie naked on a thorn bed whilst being painted. At the same time, he was beaten with the flat of the knife. In battle, the owner was not allowed to use any other weapon than the knife; he was required to walk forward towards the enemy, singing the war songs associated with the Knife Bundle and to never retreat. Little wonder that few warriors were prepared to shoulder such awesome responsibilities!

the year 1765 alone. In time, metal-bladed hatchets, mostly made by whites, acquired the name tomahawk, which was probably an anglicized version of Indian terms such as *tomahack, tommahick,* and/or *tumnahecan.*

Metal-bladed tomahawks were clearly more effective weapons than stone versions. This was because a refined metal, especially iron or steel (a commercial form of iron having a very low carbon content), was tougher than flint or jasper and also could retain its sharpened edge longer. Because of its effectiveness in hand-to-hand combat, the metal hatchet became just as popular among white settlers as among Native Americans. In fact, during the eighteenth century, all white frontiersmen, as well as most American soldiers who fought in the American Revolution, carried such hatchets. A firsthand account of a tomahawk fight during that era has survived. In the summer of 1778, David Welch, an American soldier who was fighting the British in Vermont, noticed two of Britain's Indian allies sitting beside a campfire in the woods. After creeping up on them, he drew his gun and, as he later reported:

Whilst lying thus flat on the ground, I took deliberate aim at one of the Indians and shot him dead. The other Indian instantly sprung upon his feet, seizing his gun, and started to run. Without reflecting upon the consequence, I immediately ran after him, having my gun unloaded. The Indian made but a few leaps after I started before he turned and fired upon me, but his fire missed . . . by several feet. He then dropped his gun and came at me with his tomahawk. I encountered him with my empty gun. The first blow which he aimed with his tomahawk I warded off with my gun, and in doing it I was so fortunate as to hook the deadly weapon from him. It fell upon the ground rather behind me. I was then encouraged and sprung to get the tomahawk, in which effort I succeeded. Whilst I was yet bent in picking up the toma- hawk, the Indian, who had drawn his knife, gave me a cut, giving me a deep but short wound upon my right leg a little above my knee. He then aimed a second stroke at me with the same weapon. This blow I warded off with my left hand, in doing which I received a wound between the thumb and forefinger. About the same instant, with the tomahawk I hit him a blow on the head which brought him to the ground, and with another blow after he had fallen I made sure he was beyond doing me any further harm. [11]

The Pipe Tomahawk

Such metal-bladed hatchets came in hun- dreds of different sizes and styles. By far the most popular among Native Americans across the continent was the pipe tomahawk, which the English called the "smoke toma- hawk." Because of the distinctive shape of its head, it was really two tools in one. Jutting from one side was the striking blade, which made it an instrument of warfare. On the other side of the head was the bowl of a pipe (which opened into the hollow handle). Be- cause smoking such a pipe was a traditional Indian peace ritual, the pipe tomahawk could also be used as an instrument of peace.

It remains unclear when the first pipe tom- ahawks appeared, but most historians accept

A colonial white settler and his family battle attacking Indians in this romanticized book illustration.

a date of about 1700 to 1710. Certainly by the 1750s they were in common use all across the eastern sector of the continent and after that continued to spread westward. In the late eighteenth century, a contemporary white observer of the Cherokee, who dwelled in the Southeast, commented that the pipe tomahawk "is one of their most useful pieces of field-furniture, serving all the offices of hatchet, pipe, and sword."[12] It is also unclear who first invented this durable and popular weapon. Because most of the specimens in use were made in white shops and distributed by whites, one view holds that a white person probably invented it. One expert, Richard Pohrt, disagrees, however. He suggests that the basic design of the weapon may have originated among Native Americans and that white manufacturers then copied that style to cater to Indian preferences. "It seems but a short step," Pohrt writes,

for an Indian patiently fitting a handle in a hatchet head, to realize he had the makings of a pipe stem. The addition of a pipe bowl to the . . . back of his hatchet blade would produce a dual purpose object—one that could be used for chopping or smoking.[13]

Supporting Pohrt's thesis is the fact that the most common type of wood used for the handles of pipe tomahawks—ash, usually from a sapling—was also the most common type long used by the Indians to make peace pipes. Ash "not only gave a stronger wooden stem which could take high polish," Colin Taylor explains,

but also enabled a hole to be comparatively easily bored through for use in smoking. Ash has a soft pith center which is easily removed by burning

This pipe tomahawk from an eastern woodlands tribe bears an intricate blade-carving depicting an Indian striking a white settler.

Unable to Make Gunpowder

*Although American Indians became profi-
cient with guns and learned to assemble them,
they lacked access to gunpowder. As explained
by Armstrong Starkey in* European and Native
American Warfare, *this made them very vulnerable to the whites.*

During the seventeenth century, New England Indians acquired the art of casting
bullets and making gunflints. There is evidence
that during King Philip's War [1675–1676] Indian blacksmiths became proficient in the repair of muskets and in assembling them from
parts. On the other hand, gunpowder manufacture was an extremely difficult procedure in
the seventeenth and eighteenth centuries,
one which required considerable concentra-
tions of capital and technological expertise.
Indian craftsmen could become gunsmiths,
but gunpowder was the product of an indus-
try beyond the reach of Indian societies.
While weapons could be repaired and re-
used, gunpowder was an expendable and per-
ishable commodity which only Europeans
could supply. This was a key area of Indian
military vulnerability. Tribes cut off from their
ammunition supply could quickly experience a
crisis.

or splitting the wood lengthwise, cutting out the pith and then sticking the
two pieces back together. The handle
was often decorated with heavy brass-
headed trade tacks and the lower end
covered with buckskin to facilitate a
firm grip.[14]

Matchlocks and Flintlocks

As in the case of hatchets and other weapons
with blades made of processed metals, Native
Americans first obtained firearms from early
white settlers and traders. In fact, the first
guns introduced to Indians came from French
and English trappers in the Great Lakes region in the early 1600s. One tribe in the area,
the Cree, became middlemen in a vigorous
trade in which the whites gave the Indians
guns in exchange for animal furs, which were
highly valued in Europe. This trade not only
brought the Cree prosperity; it also afforded
them unusual access to large numbers of
firearms, which in turn gave them an advantage that helped them defeat their Native
American neighbors. In the years that followed, firearms steadily spread across the
continent; by the late eighteenth century,
nearly all tribes had them.

Until the late 1700s, most of the handheld guns used by both whites and Indians were muskets. A musket was a gun
with a long barrel whose bore (inside)
had a smooth surface, hence the common
term smoothbore musket. There were two
main kinds of muskets—the matchlock
and flintlock—both of which were distributed to Indians. The first version of
the musket had appeared in Europe in the
mid- to late 1300s. It was so long and
heavy that it had to be supported by a pole
when firing and usually required two men
to operate. Smaller versions that could be
carried and fired by a single soldier came
into use in the 1400s. To fire such a
weapon, the operator touched a piece of

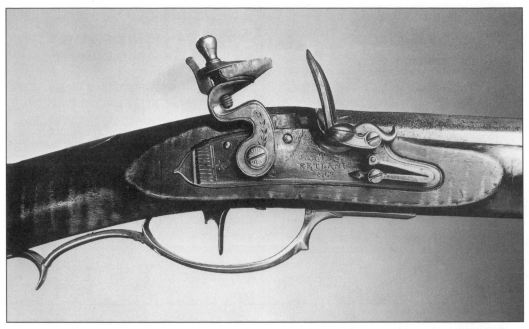

A close-up view of a flintlock mechanism shows its spring-loaded hammer primed to strike its metal plate. The sparks produced will ignite the gunpowder.

smoldering rope, the "match," to a hole in the barrel to ignite the gunpowder inside. Disadvantages of these early muskets were that they were inaccurate and took a long time to load. The matchlock mechanism, introduced in the mid- to late 1400s, was a major improvement. In the matchlock, a metal lever bolted to the top of the barrel held the smoldering match in place. When the operator pulled the trigger, a spring snapped the lever back so that the match touched and ignited a small amount of powder in a tiny pan. The flash then penetrated a hole in the barrel, igniting the powder inside and firing the gun. All of the guns that Europeans initially traded to Native Americans were matchlocks.

The next major technical innovation in musketry, the flintlock, appeared in the mid- to late 1600s. It ignited the powder in its pan with sparks from a piece of flint hitting against steel, which increased both the reliability and loading speed of the weapon. According to military historian Archer Jones,

> The flint, held by the spring-loaded hammer, struck a blow against a plate attached to the cover of the pan, opening the pan as it simultaneously caused sparks which ignited the powder and fired the musket. The mechanism proved much more reliable than the matchlock, initially firing two-thirds of the time as against the matchlock's 50 percent rate. Subsequent improvements enabled the musket to fire 85 percent of the time. The flintlock greatly increased the rate of fire, a process speeded up by the use of an oblong paper cartridge

that contained the ball and the proper amount of powder. With the old matchlock, a musketeer first filled his pan from a powderhorn; opened a small wooden cartridge and emptied its powder into the cloth from his hat; took his ramrod [a wooden or metal stick] and rammed the cloth and ball down upon it, and fastened it to the lock, ready to fire at last. With a flintlock the musketeer bit off the end of the cartridge with his teeth, retaining the ball in his mouth; used some powder from the cartridge to fill the pan and poured the remainder down the barrel, following it with the ball from his mouth and the paper of the cartridge; he then used his ramrod to drive the paper and ball down on the powder, and he was ready to fire. Instead of one round a minute, the soldier with a flintlock with paper cartridge could fire two or three or even more rounds in a minute.[15]

Another improvement in the flintlock was the use of stronger metal alloys for the barrel. This allowed for larger, more powerful powder charges, which increased the velocity of a one-ounce musket ball to about one thousand feet per second, making it more lethal than slower-moving balls.

Considering the advantages of flintlocks over matchlocks, it is not surprising that Native Americans preferred to get their hands on flintlocks whenever possible. Unfortunately for them, flintlocks were usually much more expensive to obtain. So at any given time, a tribe's supply of guns might consist of a mix of older, outdated matchlocks and a few newer flintlocks.

The Rifle and Percussion Cap

Whether they were matchlocks or flintlocks, muskets had a serious disadvantage with which whites and Indians alike had to contend. The problem stemmed from the fact that the weapon's bore was smooth. For various technical reasons, the musket ball was smaller than the bore. For example, a common British musket, the Long Land Service model, had a bore .753 inches wide. But the ball it fired was .70 inches across. The space between the edge of the ball and the inside of the barrel—in this case, .053 inches—was called windage. The problem was that the windage allowed the ball to meander from side to side as it moved down the barrel, so it exited the gun slightly off center, making it chronically inaccurate.

This drawback was largely eliminated in another kind of gun the Indians acquired from the whites—the rifle. The term rifle is derived from the weapon's "rifling," a set of spiral grooves etched into the inside walls of the barrel. When the weapon was fired, the ball spun through the grooves and exited the gun spinning; at the same time, the ball had a tight fit in the bore, almost eliminating the windage. The result was a much more accurate shot. Another advantage of the rifle, military historian Ian Hogg explains, was its

> greater range and velocity, due again to the tight fit of the ball. The musket ball's windage allowed a proportion of the propelling gas to rush past and be wasted in muzzle blast, whereas the rifle ball, firmly lodged in the rifling, sealed all the gas behind it and extracted every available scrap of performance from the powder.[16]

The first rifles appeared in the 1500s. But their manufacture required special tools and much skill, so they were not widely adopted until the 1600s. And even then they remained mainly a hunter's weapon. Early rifles, which like muskets used either a matchlock or flintlock firing mechanism, reached the American colonies in the early 1700s when German and Swiss gunsmiths emigrated across the Atlantic and set up shop. The main reason that the rifle was far less common than the less-accurate musket for so long, among both whites and Indians, was that the rifle took much longer to load. The rifleman had first to force the ball into the rifling near the gun's muzzle (the front end of the barrel), often with a mallet, and then use his ramrod (a stick) to push it farther down into the barrel. As a result, most riflemen could get off only one shot per minute, or two at best.

This situation changed dramatically with the introduction of a new firing system, based on the percussion cap, between 1807 and 1814. The cap consisted of a metal hammer that struck a metal plate when the operator pulled the trigger. The plate was coated with a chemical, potassium chlorate, that ignited on impact, firing the weapon. This innovation allowed the gun to be loaded by inserting a cartridge containing a bullet into its breech (the back end of the barrel). Eventually, repeating rifles, which used cartridges containing more than one bullet, came into use.

A Pawnee warrior aims a rifle during target practice. Through trade and other means, many Native Americans acquired rifles and became adept marksmen.

INDIANS WITH CANNONS

Handheld guns were not the only firearms that affected Native Americans in their wars with the whites. Cannons (artillery) proved potent weapons when used against Indian stockades or against frontal assaults by Indians on white forts. For the most part, Indians were unable to acquire cannons or to learn to use them. One of the few exceptions occurred in 1675, when about a hundred Susquehannock warriors defended an old European fort on the Susquehanna River in Maryland. They reinforced the wooden defensive walls, moat, and other fortifications. They also used an unknown number of Swedish-made cannons, which some white Marylanders had shown them how to operate during a siege that had taken place a few years before (at which time the Susquehannocks and Marylanders had been allies). Thanks to the cannons, in 1675 the Susquehannocks kept between 750 and 1,000 Virginia and Maryland militiamen from taking the fort by force.

Native Americans obtained some rifles through trade, others by stealing them from white farms or forts. Supply never kept up with demand, however, especially in the case of repeating rifles, which were practically as valuable as gold to both whites and Indians. So as late as the 1870s, most tribes that had not already been conquered by the whites still had to supplement their supplies of rifles with muskets.

Their Most Prestigious Weapon

The relentless white conquest of the Native Americans might not have occurred, or at least been long delayed, if most of the tribes had managed both to unite and to acquire large numbers of up-to-date guns. The fact is that the Indians did much more than simply adopt European firearms; they also rapidly mastered them and employed them with considerably more skill and accuracy than most whites, who were for the most part mediocre marksmen. (Some exceptions were professional hunters and elite army marksmen.) "Indians drew no sharp distinction between hunting and warfare," historian Armstrong Starkey points out,

and therefore trained to achieve accurate marksmanship in both. From an early age, Indian men spent their lives in the acquisition of these skills so that they became second nature. In contrast, the European peasantry were disarmed by law in most countries. When recruited as soldiers, they were not trained to fire at marks, but rather in unaimed volley fire. Destructive enough at close quarters on European battlefields, this method of fire was of little use in the woods. European settlers in North America brought with them the European way of war. While they possessed firearms for self-defense, they remained for the most part an agrarian people with little skill in hunting or marksmanship. . . . Ironically, North American Indians not only turned firearms to their own use,

Although rifles were in many ways superior to bows and arrows, most tribes retained the bow as a supplemental weapon. The warriors pictured here carry both weapons.

but became the most formidable marksmen in the seventeenth- and eighteenth-century world. The challenge that this presented to European soldiers cannot be overestimated.[17]

Indeed, Indian proficiency with muskets and rifles was one reason that these weapons came to replace the bow and arrow in both hunting and warfare in some areas. (Nevertheless, most Indian warriors remained skilled in the use of the bow, partly to supplement the use of guns and also to maintain tradition.) Other reasons for the switchover

from bows to guns included the fact that bullets were less likely to be deflected by tree branches; Indians were adept at dodging arrows but could not dodge bullets; and bullets were usually more lethal than arrows. While not discounting these reasons, Reginald Laubin favors another. "It was largely a matter of prestige," he says.

Like almost everyone else, they [the Indians] liked new things. The gun at first terrified them with its fire, smoke, and noise, but when they found they could obtain them for themselves and could handle the monsters as well as could the light-skinned newcomers, they were anxious to have them. To add to their lure, guns were very expensive, costing many pelts, which in themselves were not easy to obtain. Therefore, the man who could afford a gun was a special hunter, an exceptional trapper, and most important, an admired warrior.[18]

It turned out to be a tragic twist of fate that the Indians acquired the weapon they found most alluring and prestigious from the people who ultimately destroyed their way of life.

CHAPTER THREE

Defensive Weapons and Tactics

To counter the effects of offensive weapons, Native Americans, like the Europeans and other peoples around the globe, developed various defensive weapons, measures, and tactics. These included body armor, shields, and fortifications. In many ways, the Indian versions strongly resembled those that had long been used in Europe and the Near East.

Wooden Body Armor

Perhaps the principal difference between Native American and European body armor was that the Indians used mainly wood and other natural materials instead of processed metals. Only after contact with whites and other foreigners did a few tribes begin reinforcing their armor with iron strips.[19] And this occurred mainly in areas where wood was not readily available or abundant, such as in the cold, icy regions of Canada and Alaska where the Inuit and Eskimo dwelled. These and some other Native American peoples also fashioned armor from materials such as bone and ivory. A complete ivory cuirass (chest protector)

made by the Aleut, linguistic relatives of the Eskimo, came into the possession of the governor of Alaska (then under Russian control) in 1836 and remains in a remarkable state of preservation. It is fashioned of several dozen ivory strips varying in length from four to nine inches, all tied snugly together with pieces of rawhide.

For the most part, though, the two most common materials Indians used for making body armor were wood and multilayered animal hides. Typical of the wooden variety is a surviving cuirass of the Tlingit, who inhabited the continent's northwest coastal region. The front section is composed of ten vertical wooden slats bound together with strips of animal sinew and rawhide. Missing now is a painted crest that adorned the central portion. Attached to the end slats are sections made of lightweight, somewhat flexible wooden rods, also placed vertically. These sections fell under the wearer's armpits, allowing his arms more range of movement than would have been possible if the whole cuirass had been made of the more rigid slats. Wide rawhide strips attached to the top-front of the armor ran back over the wearer's shoulder and connected to the back section, which was made of slats like the front.

Such chest protectors were sometimes supplemented with neck collars and helmets. These were made from bundles of wooden rods (smaller versions of those used under the arms in the cuirass) or from a single, carved piece of wood. Some Tlingit helmets even had movable visors similar to those on the metal helmets of medieval European knights. An eighteenth-century drawing made by a Spanish explorer shows a Tlingit warrior wearing such a combination of cuirass, neck guard, and visored helmet. This warrior's cuirass extends downward past the middle of the thigh, and he wears an ankle-length leather skirt beneath it to protect the

lower legs. Such an outfit clearly afforded the wearer excellent protection against enemy rocks and arrows.

Native suits of armor like those of the Tlingit strongly resembled the mostly metal armored suits worn by early Spanish explorers. This naturally raises the question of whether the Indians adopted such armor from the Spanish or developed the idea on their own. The answer seems to be that both scenarios occurred, depending on the region. The Indians of the Southwest and Florida, for instance, had very early contacts with the Spanish and soon afterward developed elaborate armored suits. As Colin Taylor puts it, "It is probable that the use of this type of protective weaponry . . . was adopted and modified by the . . . [Indians] utilizing the native materials readily available to them." [20]

 # WEAPONS OF THE NEZ PERCÉ

Edward S. Curtis (1868–1952) was a photographer and ethnologist who carefully documented the lives and customs of more than eighty Native American tribes west of the Mississippi River. In 1930, after more than thirty years of work, he completed his masterwork, The North American Indian. *Each of its twenty volumes contains some three hundred pages of text and seventy-five photographs taken by Curtis himself. This excerpt from volume eight describes some of the offensive and defensive weapons of the Nez Percé, who lived in the northwestern United States.*

Bows about three feet in length and of great strength were fashioned from mountainsheep horn, and were either of one piece or of two pieces spliced. Red cedar and sy-

ringa also were used. All well-made bows were strengthened with a backing of several layers of sinew. Arrows were principally of syringa. Flint-headed spears were sometimes used in war, also clubs consisting of a spherical stone wrapped in rawhide and provided with a wooden handle; such a weapon was called *kaplafs.* An effective armor was manufactured of rawhide taken from the neck of the bull-elk. This shirt of mail, called *tukupailakt,* protected the upper part of the body, had half-length sleeves, and was fastened at the front with thongs. The Nez Percé shield, which was used only by war-leaders and their principal followers, was made of doubled rawhide of the elk, unshrunken, and stretched over a wooden hoop; it sometimes bore painted representations of the war exploits of its owner.

This crest, which once decorated the front of a set of Native American body armor, has been carved and painted to represent a shark's face.

On the other hand, strong evidence suggests that some Native American tribes developed various versions of body armor on their own, either prior to or after the appearance of white Europeans. The Huron and Iroquois in the Northeast and some tribes in Virginia also used elaborate armor composed of wooden rods and slats. A European drawing made before 1660 shows a Huron warrior wearing such an outfit. Moreover, early white settlers who lacked armor sometimes adopted already existing native versions, instead of the other way around. In about 1608, for instance, Captain John Smith, the famous cofounder of the English colony of Jamestown, Virginia, found himself under attack by a local tribe; another tribe, which was on friendly terms with Smith and his people, helped him and his men don Indian-made wooden armor. It was so effective that, in the words of one of the white participants, it "securely beat back the savages from off the plain without [our receiving] any hurt."[21]

Hide Armor

The other common kind of Indian armor, made from layers of animal hides, was used by tribes in many parts of North America. The Tlingit and other northwestern tribes used hides, sometimes by themselves and other times beneath their wooden armor to double the amount of protection. The Shoshone, Pawnee, and several other Plains tribes used hide armor, too, as did the Navajo in the Southwest and the Mohawk, who dwelled in the East near Lake Ontario.

Typically, such armor consisted of two or more layers of hide stitched together with rawhide strips. Elk hide was widely used, although hides from moose, buffalo, and other large mammals were also employed in various areas. The front of such a leather cuirass was usually elaborately decorated. Sometimes faces (of people, spirits, or gods) or designs were painted on in bright colors; other decorations included rows of sharks' teeth, bones from various animals, buttons, and even metal coins acquired through trade with non-Indians.

This Plains warrior wears hide armor consisting of several layers. His shield provides added protection.

Hide armor was also used to protect horses, usually by Plains tribes such as the Shoshone. In 1805, Lewis and Clark, who had been sent by President Thomas Jefferson to explore the western part of the continent, witnessed the use of horse armor, writing in their journal,

> They [the Indians] have a kind of armor something like a coat of mail, which is formed from a great many folds of dressed antelope-skins, united by means of a mixture of glue and sand. With this they cover their own bodies and those of their horses, and find it impervious to the arrow. [22]

The use of such horse armor did not spread very far from the regions of major contact between Indians and the early Spanish explorers. So, the Indians probably borrowed the idea from the whites. However, another version of horse armor used on the plains may well have been of native origin. It consisted of a single, thin layer of rawhide decorated with four shieldlike disks. It could not have afforded the horse much physical protection, so it was likely meant to offer symbolic, spiritual protection by invoking the protective powers of a sky god.

In general, Native American body armor was reasonably effective against most Indian offensive weapons. However, it was far less effective against bullets. Consequently, as guns spread across the continent, the use of armor steadily declined.

Shields

Many Indian warriors carried shields, either in addition to or instead of body armor. The most common type of shield in use through-out the Midwest, West, and Northeast was circular and made of tree bark, wood, or dried animal hides, or sometimes a combination of these materials. A style popular with the Comanche, a tribe living in the West and Southwest, was made from two pieces of rawhide laced together around a wooden hoop; the space in the middle was stuffed with feathers, grass, horse hair, or some other pliable material to help blunt the momentum of a club or arrow. Most such shields were about three feet in diameter and featured a neck strap that allowed a warrior to carry his shield on his side, shoulder, or back. This relieved some of the burden of carrying the object for long distances. Almost always, a warrior wrapped his shield in a protective buckskin cover when it was not in use.

Although circular shields were the norm, a few other types were used. Some very ancient examples from northwestern North America were rectangular or oblong. And some early Spanish explorers described large shields that covered a warrior's whole body. An eighteenth-century Native American recollection of such shields has survived. Saukamappee, an elder of the Piegan tribe of the northern plains, was present when Piegan warriors confronted a force of enemy Shoshone in 1720. "Both parties made a great show of their numbers," he remembered,

> and I thought that they were more numerous than ourselves. After some singing and dancing they sat down on the ground, and placed their large shields before them, which covered them. We did the same, but our shields were not so many, and some of our shields had to shelter two men. [23]

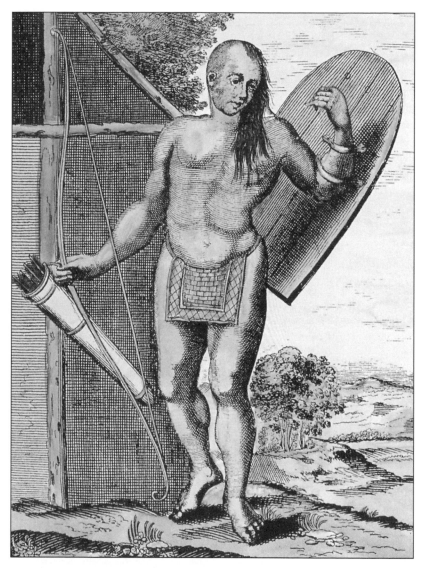

A warrior native to southern Canada carries an oblong wooden shield. Such shields were usually wrapped in buckskin when not in use.

Whatever their shape and size, Indian shields were seen by their owners as more than just utilitarian. They were also thought to impart supernatural protection to their owners. Thus, both a shield and its cover were usually embellished with designs representing or meant to invoke the powers of various spirits, or earth, animal, or sky gods. In keeping with this symbolic or sacred function of shields, their production often involved a ceremony. George Catlin, the foremost chronicler-artist of the American Indians in the nineteenth century, observed and described the so-called smoking of the shield ceremony:

> A young man about to construct him a shield digs a hole of two feet in

TECHNIQUES OF PAINTING WEAPONS

One of the most important aspects of making Indian defensive weapons like shields was painting them with designs, which often had spiritual as well as decorative functions. In this tract from his informative Atlas of the North American Indian, *historian Carl Waldman discusses the paints and techniques used by Native American artisans.*

Native North Americans . . . extracted their paints from a variety of raw materials—earth with iron ore for reds, yellow, and browns; copper ore for green and blue; soot or graphite for black; and clay, limestone, and gypsum for white—and used them to decorate tepees, shields, pottery, ceremonial objects, etc. Paint was applied with fingers, sticks, brushes, or sprayed from the mouth, and was often held in shells. Body paint was also used for symbolic purposes; i.e., to indicate social position or an intent to make war. Indians extracted dyes from plant sources—berries, roots, barks—to color textiles, basket materials, and quills.

War paint decorates the weapons and body of Last Horse, a Sioux warrior.

depth, in the ground, and as large in diameter as he designs to make his shield. In this [hole] he builds a fire, and over it, a few inches higher than the ground, he stretches the rawhide horizontally over the fire, with little pegs driven through holes made near the edges of the skin. This skin is at first twice as large as the size of the required shield. But having got his particular and best friends . . . into a ring, to dance and sing around it, and solicit the Great Spirit to instill into it the power to protect him harmless against his enemies, he spreads over it the glue, which is rubbed and dried in as the skin is heated; and a second [warrior] busily drives other . . . pegs, inside of those in the ground, as they are gradually giving way and being pulled up by the contraction of the skin. By this curious process . . . the skin is kept tight while it contracts to one half of its size, taking up the glue and increasing in thickness until it is rendered as thick and hard as required . . . when the dance ceases, and the fire is put out. When it is cooled and cut into the shape that he desires, it is often painted with his . . . totem [spiritual symbol] upon it.[24]

When used in combination with clubs, hatchets, and other handheld weapons, or against enemy arrows, Indian shields were highly effective defensive weapons. However, like Native American body armor, they provided little protection against bullets, so after the adoption of guns by Indians, shields became less common.

Fortifications

Another defensive measure employed by some Native American tribes, principally in the Southwest and eastern and midwestern woodlands, was the fortification of villages

A white settler named Johannes Staden drew this picture of a Native American fort. The timber palisade strongly resembles the kind erected by white settlers and soldiers.

DEFENSES SET ABLAZE

One common method Indians used to capture a fortified position was to burn it. Here, from his Flintlock and Tomahawk, *former Vanderbilt University scholar Douglas Leach describes an attack by the Nipmucks, a New England tribe, against some English who had fortified themselves in a house.*

When bullets alone failed to overcome the garrison, the Indians resorted to fire. They shot flaming arrows into the roof of the house, but the people inside cut holes in the roof and extinguished the flames before they could spread. The Indians piled combustible material such as hay against one corner of the building, and set it on fire, but some of the English dashed from their shelter and put out the blaze. Once again the Nipmucks tried, this time by lighting their fire against the wall of the building, and then concentrating their strength in the vicinity of the door to prevent another sortie, but the desperate defenders broke down part of the wall in order to extinguish the fire. Next, the warriors built an ingenious mobile torch. This consisted of a barrel to which were attached a pair of extremely long shafts constructed by splicing many long poles end to end. The shafts rested upon a series of paired wheels which had been taken from captured farm vehicles. By pushing on the extreme ends of the two shafts the Indians could move the barrel up against the wall of the garrison house, without themselves coming too near the guns of the English. However, a sudden rainstorm soaked the combustibles, and temporarily saved the garrison from the flames.

One tribe attacks another with fire arrows in this sixteenth-century drawing. Some Indians also used this technique against white forts and villages.

and ceremonial centers. Some of these defenses were quite elaborate and strongly resembled the wooden stockades and other forts built by Europeans. The most common feature was a tall palisade, a wall made of vertical timber poles planted deep in the ground and lashed together with thick strips of rawhide. Sometimes earthen embankments were constructed outside the palisade to provide an extra defensive position for the villagers; they first manned these mounds to keep the enemy at bay, and then, if necessary, retreated behind the palisade. In addition, moatlike ditches were sometimes dug outside of palisades to discourage attackers.

In the East, such defenses surrounded a whole village, which was often made up of several dozen bark longhouses grouped around a central square. The intent was to protect most or all of the members of the tribe from attack by warriors of a neighboring tribe. By contrast, fortifications in the Southwest were apparently designed to protect a central ceremonial center. According to Norman Bancroft-Hunt, a noted scholar of North American Indians,

A concentration of power at the temple is interesting, because many of the principal towns of the southeastern tribes were religious sanctuaries as well as being combined military and administrative centers from which the chiefs and priests could exert authority over smaller outlying hamlets occupied by subject tribes. The descriptions we have suggest these towns were protected by palisades, ditches and earth embankments, and sometimes even by

moats, with the house of the chief, the temples of the priests and the dwellings of other dignitaries raised on earthen mounds protected by secondary palisades or walls. By far the larger part of the population lived outside these massive fortifications, and the only permanent occupancy was by an exclusive class of civil, military, and religious leaders, who were guarded by warrior societies whose specific function was to protect the nobility and priests. Other people only came here when summoned by the chief or to observe and participate in ceremonies conducted at the temples. [25]

Although such fortifications were often effective in the short run, in the case of a prolonged siege by another tribe, they actually worked in favor of the attackers. The attackers would erect small temporary forts around the fortified village (a siege technique also employed by the ancient Greeks and Romans) and settle down to starve out the defenders. As Bancroft-Hunt points out, the entrance in the palisade was usually quite narrow and permitted "only two or three people access at a time." The disadvantage of such a small passageway was that it

created a prison for its occupants, since a few men could easily prevent warriors in any large number from leaving the town to counter-attack. This made the siege doubly effective. Not only was access to water denied, but the town's inhabitants had to be constantly vigilant whereas their

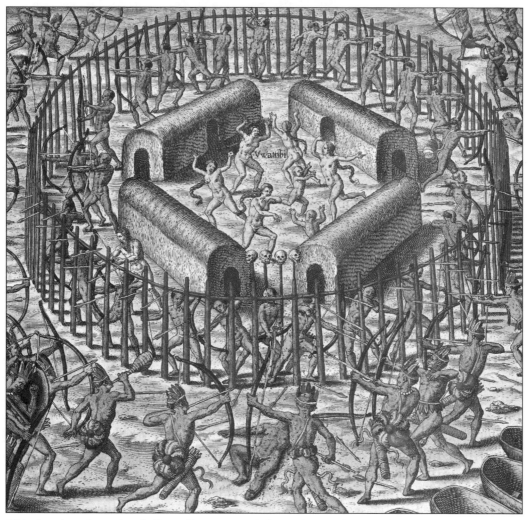

This drawing of warring Indian tribes was made by a white explorer in the 1500s. The palisade surrounding a group of bark longhouses was typical of several eastern tribes.

opponents needed to keep only a minimum force in the field. Secure in their temporary forts, most of the attacking party could relax in relative comfort, sending out fresh warriors from time to time to replace those attacking the town, and simply wait for their opponents to be worn down through lack of water and sleep.[26]

The same delicate balance between safety and peril existed when Indians attacked white settlers who had taken refuge behind a palisade. Most of the time, Indians did not think it was smart to risk a frontal assault, especially if the whites had cannons. So as long as the whites remained behind the walls and had enough food, water, and ammunition, they were relatively safe. However, these provisions usually ran out faster than anyone had expected. Also, settlers tended to worry about their homes, fields, and livestock, which were likely in Indian hands on the outside. So, they sometimes unwisely ventured outside the walls, only to fall into a deadly ambush set up by the besiegers. The line between defensive and offensive warfare is sometimes a thin one, and Native Americans were highly adept at crossing it when the need and opportunity arose.

CHAPTER FOUR

Horses Transform Warfare on the Plains

For many people, the image of the Native Americans of the Great Plains both hunting bison (or buffalo) and fighting on horseback has become symbolic of American Indian culture in general. However, this popular image is both artificial and misleading. The horse was not indigenous to North America, and the so-called horse and bison culture of the Great Plains developed only after early white settlers introduced the horse to the native inhabitants of the plains. That culture was therefore a very late and short-lived phenomenon that lasted only about three or four generations and was not indicative of Indian civilization in general.

The first horses in the region appeared in the Southwest and southern Great Plains in about 1600, when the Spanish began settling in New Mexico. At first, the Spanish carefully guarded their horses, which were an extremely valuable and hard-to-replace commodity. They even instituted laws prohibiting the sale of horses to Indians.

But through illicit trade, theft, or both, some nearby tribes soon acquired the animals, including the Apache, who had horses at least by 1630. After 1680, horses and knowledge of how to break and train them rapidly spread northward into the plains. By 1700, the Comanche had them; by 1720, the Shoshone, Nez Percé, and eastern Ute; by 1740 or so, the Cheyenne, Arapaho, Kansas, Crow, Blackfeet, and Lakota (Sioux); and by 1770, the Assiniboin and Cree. The horse transformed the lives of these peoples almost overnight (in historical terms). The horse became, in Paul Carlson's words,

the most important vehicle of transportation, medium of exchange, and regulator of economic values and social status. It came to exercise considerable influence over the minds of the people, altering world views, religious practices, subsistence patterns, and even the traditional nature and ideology of warfare.[27]

THE LUXURY OF WASTE

The adoption of the horse by the Plains Indians, as well as other commodities introduced to them by whites, brought profound changes in native culture, as explained here by Peter Farb (from his Man's Rise to Civilization*).*

No longer were just stray or stampeded bison taken, but the herds were pursued on swift horses, and the choicest animals killed. No longer was the whole animal utilized for raw materials, . . . but the Indians could now afford the luxury of waste. They stocked the tipi with supplies for the future: meat dried in the sun (jerkee), or else pounded and mixed with fat and berries to become pemmican. Even though most of the plains Indians never saw a white close-up until their swift decline, his influence was felt profoundly as his goods and trade articles flowed westward across the plains by barter from one tribe to another. Tipis almost twenty-five feet in diameter were filled to overflowing with newfound riches. An economic revolution, for which the Indians' traditions had not prepared them, took place. The women no longer toiled in the fields—for gardening was not as profitable as hunting, nor could it be practiced in the presences of nomadic horsemen—and they stopped making pottery because brass kettles were obtained from whites. Permanent villages disappeared, and with them went the elaborate customs and crafts, [and] rules for marriage and residence.

In this fanciful scene, an elderly warrior gazes at a buffalo skull and conjures up a vision of the spirits of long-dead hunters and herds.

Before the Horse

To understand the extent of the changes the horse brought about in Plains Indian warfare, it is first necessary to consider how the region's precontact inhabitants hunted and fought. (To these people, hunting and fighting were closely interrelated.) Put simply, they did both on foot. They were mainly agriculturalists, subsisting primarily on crops such as corn, beans, and squash. Meat from bison was only an occasional supplement to the diet and seen as far less important than the hides, sinew, bones, and other products obtained from these large animals. The Spanish explorer Francisco Coronado penetrated the plains as far north as Kansas in the 1500s and later commented on the degree to which the natives depended on these products:

> With the skins they build their houses; with the skins they clothe and show themselves; from the skins they make ropes and also obtain wool. With the sinews they make threads, with which they sew their clothes and also their tents. From the bones they shape awls. The dung they use for firewood, since there is no other fuel in that land. The bladders they use as jugs and drinking containers. [28]

One good hunt could provide enough bison products to meet a tribe's needs for many months. So, the typical tribe conducted such hunts only once or twice a year. Because they did not have horses, the hunters had to resort to less mobile means of trapping and killing their prey. In one method, known as the foot surround, a long line of people encircled a group of grazing bison and slowly tightened the circle; they then used spears and arrows to dispatch the animals. Another technique was to trap the bison by setting fire to the grass around them and then move in for the kill. Impounding was yet another method. "When impounding bison," Carlson explains,

> the people drove a herd into the wide end of a funnel formed by two lines of camouflaged hunters. As the animals approached, the hunters, with sometimes women and children participating, one by one came from hiding to frighten the bison through the narrowing trap into a stout enclosure of logs

A drawing made in 1758 shows Indians using a foot surround to hunt a deer.

HORSES CAUSE SOCIAL CHANGE

In this excerpt from his book about the Plains Indians, Paul Carlson outlines some of the major social and economic effects that the adoption of horses had on their cultures.

Horses altered economic concepts, established great differences in wealth and correlative prestige, and, in what once had been an egalitarian society [one based on equality], created socioeconomic classes based on wealth, particularly horses. Village paupers, those people with only one or two horses, had to walk when the camp moved.

People of wealth owned many horses, with individual herds sometimes numbering one hundred or more head. A man with horses could buy ceremonial privileges or enhance his social position by giving them away. A young man in love, through a male family member who conducted negotiations with the prospective bride's family, might offer several horses to the father of a beautiful and virtuous girl he wanted to marry. As time passed, then, accumulation of horses (property wealth), rather than the sharing of property, began to define one's social position.

and brush at the spout, sometimes two or more feet below the funnel. Once they had the bison impounded, they might butcher the entire herd, perhaps netting as many as three hundred to six hundred animals. [29]

Like hunting, fighting on the plains before the introduction of the horse was influenced by the subsistence needs and habits of the people. Because they relied mainly on crops for food, most tribes were not nomadic; instead, they lived in settled villages surrounded by large tracts of open territory. The territories of other tribes were usually located at quite a distance. This tended to limit the frequency of warfare among tribes.

Moreover, such fighting was almost always limited to a tribe's immediate neighbor or neighbors. To walk hundreds of miles, fight a battle, and then walk all the way home again was too difficult and time-consuming for people who were living at subsistence level. The motivation for intertribal fighting was another factor that limited its scope. In general, pre-horse plains warfare was driven more by psychological and ritualistic needs than by desire for conquest or gaining spoils. As former Smithsonian scholar Peter Farb puts it,

> The plains Indians fought not to win territory or to enslave other tribes. . . . External strife served to unify the tribe internally. A tribe . . . [that was] unified only by non-kin [social groups], needed a common enemy as a rationale for its existence. . . . [Also] war was regarded as a game in which the players might win status. [30]

Generally, this ritualistic kind of warfare was characterized by lines of warriors facing each other on the open plain. One group would hurl insults or fire arrows at the other at a distance; less frequently, hand-to-hand combat, which was more deadly, would occur. As a rule, battles were over quickly, casualties were few, and villages remained intact.

After the Plains Indians adopted horses, the need to control grasslands to maintain these animals became crucial. Here, warriors of one tribe have seized the grasslands of another.

Acquiring Wealth and Exploiting Territory

Most of these age-old patterns of hunting and fighting changed radically when the Plains Indians adopted the horse. Hunter-warriors now had the means to chase down individual bison and kill them as they ran. This was much more energy efficient for the Indians and allowed them to range much farther from home in search of prey. In fact, there was no longer any need for permanent villages. Hunting became more frequent and

meat came to replace most vegetables in the diet, so hunters crowded out farmers or the farmers became hunters themselves. In addition, as the bison herds moved from place to place, the Indians started to follow them, adopting more of a nomadic existence.

This enhanced mobility based on the horse affected social customs, especially those concerned with warfare, in numerous ways. For one thing, it was now easier for a tribe to travel farther and attack more distant tribes. Also, there was now significant motivation for such expeditions. Before, no Plains tribe had wealth of any consequence, so warriors did not usually attack and loot other villages. But now, because horses were difficult to obtain and time-consuming to train, they were extremely valuable and became highly coveted. As a result, wealth came to be measured by horse ownership, and horse-stealing raids on rival villages became the central factor in intertribal conflicts on the plains. "Property wealth, measured in numbers of horses," Carlson writes,

> assumed significance in that a wealthy man must be a successful hunter or warrior. Wealth validated bravery, for through successful hunting and raiding a man obtained new wealth in the form of horses and goods. It also became tied to status in that one might improve one's social position by an unselfish sense of sharing, even to the extent of giving away personal possessions. More-

over, because socioeconomic values emphasized generosity . . . the more horses one gave away, the higher one rose in the status system.[31]

The need to exploit territory also became a prime motivation for waging war after the introduction of the horse. Specifically, the availability of grasslands proved to be a crucial factor in the communal and social patterns of the horse and bison culture. According to Carlson,

> Horses, like bison, consumed large amounts of grass for sustenance. Because the grazing requirements of their mounts led Indian people to seek camps that would provide adequate forage for their large herds, good horse pasture became as vital as good hunting territory. Although other factors (such as bison grazing patterns, spiritual needs, and cosmological views) were involved in the dynamics

A SPARSE POPULATION, FEW WARRIORS

Even at its height, in the mid-1800s, the number of warriors the horse and bison culture of the Great Plains was able to field at any given time was relatively low, especially in comparison to the size of the armies the United States was able to field. Scholars Robert Utley and Wilcomb Washburn (from Indian Wars) *explain:*

The plains culture required a vast territory for a sparse population. Altogether the plains tribes counted no more than seventy-

five thousand people. In contrast, the so-called Five Civilized Tribes—Cherokee, Creek, Choctaw, Chickasaw, Seminole—moved by the United States government from eastern homes to . . . Oklahoma, numbered eighty-four thousand, a population that yielded about four thousand fighting men. Given the wide dispersion of these tribes, such figures belie today's set-piece motion picture and television scenes depicting hordes of charging warriors from which the popular image of the Indian wars is drawn.

of social organization, many people, in order to ensure adequate forage for their ponies, separated into smaller (family, clan, or band) hunting units for much of the year especially in winter when grass was scarce. They organized into larger (band or tribal) units in early summer when grass, lush and plentiful, could support the intense grazing of large numbers of horses.[32]

Because they had become nomadic, the Plains tribes searched out and exploited numerous individual tracts of grassland. When one tribe infringed on another's recently established turf, this often led to open fighting.

The World's Greatest Horsemen

These more frequent, larger intertribal conflicts were all the more unusual when one considers how similar the cultures of the tribes had become, again mainly because of the horse. Before the introduction of that animal, only a few tribes inhabited the open areas of the so-called Great Basin of the American West. The majority of the tribes lived on the fringes in diverse environments, and, overall, their customs and beliefs, including those regarding hunting and fighting, differed in varying degrees. Then the horse appeared and drew many of the fringe tribes into the open plains. All of the tribes in the region came to use horses in basically the same manner and adopted similar social customs relating to the horse. So by about 1800, almost all of the distinct differences among these groups disappeared. "Of course, differences apparent to the trained

eye of the anthropologist still existed," says Farb.

Yet it is remarkable that a people from the eastern forests and another from the Great Basin of the west, two thousand miles away, should within only a few generations have become so nearly identical. Even more remarkable, this homogeneity [sameness] was achieved with great speed, was not imposed on unwilling people by a more powerful group, and was done in the absence of a common tongue—save for "sign language," the lingua franca [common language] of the Plains tribes.[33]

Of the many traits the tribes of the horse and bison culture shared, exploitation of the horse for both hunting and fighting was, of course, the most central. Unlike the whites, the Plains Indians did more than simply use horses to help accomplish these tasks. The warriors of the plains elevated the skill and art of riding to a level far beyond that ever achieved by whites. This made these Indians extremely formidable fighters against both other Indians and whites; in fact, if the whites had not had superior technology and firepower, it is entirely feasible that superior Indian horsemanship might have helped to delay or even prevent the white conquest of the Plains tribes. In his nineteenth-century travels on the plains, George Catlin observed this phenomenal skill among Comanche warriors, later calling them "the most extraordinary horsemen that I have yet seen in all my travels, and I doubt . . . whether any people in the world can surpass them." According to Catlin's riveting account,

This Native American pictograph, a painting done on rocks or hides, captures the high degree of riding skill acquired by many Plains warriors.

Amongst their feats of riding, there is one that has astonished me more than anything of the kind I have ever seen, or expect to see, in my life—a stratagem of war, learned and practiced by every young man in the tribe; by which he is able to drop his body upon the side of his horse at the instant he is passing, effectually screened from his enemies' weapons as he lays in a horizontal position behind the body of his horse, with his heel hanging over the horse's back; by which he has the power of throwing himself up again, and changing to the other side of the horse if necessary. In this wonderful condition, he will hang whilst his horse is at fullest speed, carrying with him his bow and his shield, and also his long lance of fourteen feet in length, all or either of which he will wield upon his enemy as he passes; rising and throwing his arrows over the horse's back, or with equal ease and equal success under the horse's neck. This astonishing feat which the young men have been repeatedly playing off to our surprise as well as amusement, whilst they have been galloping about in front of our tents, completely puzzled the whole of us; and appeared to be the result of magic, rather than of skill acquired by practice. I had several times great curiosity to approach them, to ascertain by what means their bodies

Scholar and artist George Catlin described at length his astonishment at seeing Comanche horsemen drop down onto one side of their mounts to protect themselves from enemy attack.

could be suspended in this manner, where nothing could be seen but the heel hanging over the horse's back. In these endeavors I was continually frustrated, until one day I coaxed a young fellow up within a little distance of me, by offering him a few plugs of tobacco, and he in a moment solved the difficulty, so far as to render it apparently more feasible than before; yet leaving it one of the most extraordinary results of practice and persevering endeavors. I found on examination, that a shorthair halter was passed around under the neck of the horse, and both ends tightly braided into the mane, on the withers, leaving a loop to hang under the neck, and against the breast, which, being caught up in the hand, makes a sling into which the elbow falls, taking the weight of the body on the middle of the upper arm. Into this loop the rider drops suddenly and fearlessly, leaving his heel to hang over the back of the horse, to steady him, and also to restore him when he wishes to regain his upright position on the horse's back. Besides this wonderful art, these people have several other feats of horsemanship, which they are continually showing off, which are pleasing and extraordinary, and of which they seem very proud. A people who spend so very great a part of their lives actually on their horses' backs must needs become exceedingly expert in every thing that pertains to riding—to war, or to the chase. [34]

The Final Defensive

Unfortunately for the Plains Indians, the whites did have superior technology and guns. This reality was a major factor in the ultimate white conquest of the plains in the second half of the nineteenth century. The results of this conquest were tragic. The horse and bison culture that had appeared suddenly only a few generations before and developed with astonishing speed now declined and collapsed just as quickly. Horses had transformed the warfare of the plains, making intertribal wars more common and individual warriors more formidable than ever before. Yet in the final reckoning, fighting skill and bravery could not stand up to the huge numbers of whites heading west and the massive industrial base that supplied these settlers and soldiers with advanced weaponry. Farb eloquently describes the doomed Plains Indians on the final defensive:

A wagon train of white settlers make camp. The onrush of white civilization swept the horse and bison culture away.

[American] troops pursued them mercilessly from waterhole to waterhole; their women and children were slaughtered before their eyes, their encampments and their riches burned. The glory and the poetry had gone out of the Plains Indians. Mighty chiefs emerged from hiding as miserable fugitives, hungry and without bullets for their guns. The survivors, like so many cattle, were herded onto reservations, where rough handling, cheap whiskey, starvation, exposure, and disease severely depleted their numbers. [35]

CHAPTER FIVE

When Indians Fought Indians

Depictions of Native American warriors and warfare in movies and art usually show fighting between Indians and whites in various parts of the American frontier. Often, the Indians are depicted as basically peaceful people whose traditionally tranquil lives are disrupted by warlike, land-hungry white settlers and soldiers. These images can be misleading. Although whites were often warlike, the reality is that most Native Americans were warlike, too. In fact, warfare was an accepted part of Indian life, and most of the wars and battles fought by Indians were against other Indians, even during their three centuries of struggle against white civilization.

During the many centuries before the coming of the whites, Native Americans established various tactics and modes of fighting one another. These tactics sometimes varied from region to region, and the differences were often influenced by local geography, climate, and availability of materials for making weapons. Later, Indians employed some of these same tactics against whites (although they also adopted new ones such as using guns and fighting on horseback). The Indians also developed complex rituals and ceremonies surrounding intertribal warfare. These frequently became as important as or even more important than actual combat and killing.

Motivations for Fighting

Intertribal warfare had numerous causes, both unrelated and related to contacts with white civilization. Before the appearance of whites in North America or at least before various tribes began to feel the pressures of encroaching white settlers, Native American conflicts were not usually political in nature. The desire for permanent conquest, acquisition of another people's territory, and consolidation of enormous military and political power were concepts quite common in Europe, but they were very rare among North American Indians. (Acquisition and defense of grasslands for horses by Plains tribes was a notable exception to the rule.) Most tribes did have well-defined,

Indian warriors display scalp trophies taken in combat during a celebration of victory over a neighboring tribe.

traditional territories with more or less recognized boundaries. Local spirits and gods were seen to exist with these areas, helping to reinforce the unique identities of individual tribes. But these areas were usually relatively small and as a rule did not share boundaries with neighboring tribal areas. That left considerable open spaces between, as Tom Holm explains:

> Territories surrounding [traditional tribal] lands were shared hunting grounds or ranges, claimed by numerous groups. In effect, they were no man's lands, owned by no one but used by all. Tribal warriors might meet in pitched battles or intercept another tribe's raiding party in these

neutral lands; but colonizing them, even for the sake of defense, would have been an unwarranted disruption of the natural order, necessitating a redefinition of the tribe's identity.[36]

Because gaining territory was usually not a motivating factor, Indian wars tended to be both localized and small-scale. One motivation for fighting was intertribal rivalry. Each of two tribes might feel that the other was exploiting more than its fair share of game in nearby neutral hunting grounds, so they would periodically fight. The object, however, was to chastise the enemy and restore the natural balance rather than gain sole control of the hunting grounds. Another common cause of intertribal warfare was feuding—for instance, to get revenge for the killing of one's relatives. Some Indians also attacked their neighbors to seize captives. The Aztec (who inhabited Mexico) killed war captives in religious sacrifices; the Iroquois adopted them into the tribe to replace deceased members. In addition, many tribes viewed war as a sacred activity inspired and expected by their gods.

The reasons that Indians fought other Indians remained in effect after the appearance of whites. But new and very potent reasons were introduced. Increasing pressures from the advance of white civilization caused changes in Indian cultures that often ignited intertribal animosities that might not otherwise have existed. Utley and Washburn describe some of these changes:

> Like the plains Indians, the tribes of desert, mountain, and basin at the midpoint of the nineteenth century lived in a world still basically Indian.

The white intrusions along the coast or up the river valleys and other trade routes had not disrupted the main patterns of Indian life or altered the main Indian relationships with one another. Even so, again like the plains Indians, few remained untouched by white influences. Many had incorporated the horse and gun into their scheme of life, along with a variety of other useful innovations. Many were occasionally demoralized by the white man's whisky and devastated by the white man's diseases. Some had been displaced from traditional ranges by the pressures, direct or indirect, of the white advance.[37]

Those tribes that were displaced in this manner were almost always thrown into contact with other tribes, who often became their rivals and enemies. Moreover, this process

---

 # A TRIBE THAT DID NOT FIGHT

Although the vast majority of North American Indian tribes regularly engaged in warfare, at least one did not. Before the coming of the whites, the Shoshone refrained from making war, as Peter Farb recounts here from his acclaimed book about the rise of Indian cultures.

The explanation lies not in some superior Shoshone ethic or in their being Noble Red Men, but in more practical matters. The Shoshone did not wage war because they had no reason to. They had no desire to gain military honors, for these were meaningless in their kind of society [a very simple one based completely on mutual cooperation]. They had no territories to defend, for a territory is valuable only at those times when it is producing food, and those were precisely the times when the Shoshone cooperated, rather than made war. Even if they had wanted to steal from richer neighboring Indians, they lacked both the weapons and a society sufficiently complex to be organized for concerted action. Whenever other Indians invaded their lands and attacked them, Shoshone did not fight back but simply ran away and hid.

sometimes resulted in one tribe actually displacing another; the displaced tribe then moved into another's territory with similar results. Peter Farb gives this example:

> The French encouraged warfare between the Ojibway [originally inhabiting Michigan] and surrounding groups; the Ojibway spread westward and displaced Siouan groups, which migrated westward and southward to the plains; there the Sioux displaced Hidasta and Mandan, who in turn stirred up the Cheyenne and others. The whole unreal situation was very much like a series of balls caroming [bouncing] off one another and resulting in new rebounds. [38]

Common Warrior Ideals

Regardless of the reasons that Indians fought one another or the cultural differences and animosities that set various tribes apart, almost all Native Americans shared some fundamen-

As whites moved west they displaced Native American tribes, which in turn made war on and displaced other tribes.

THE LINE BETWEEN WAR AND MURDER

As scholar Armstrong Starkey points out in this excerpt from his book about Native American warfare, many Indian tribes did not draw the European distinction between murder and deaths that occurred on the battlefield.

The Algonquian peoples believed that there were two kinds of killings: those at the hands of enemies and those at the hands of allies. If the killer belonged to an allied group, his family and community expected that the dead would be "covered" with appropriate compensation and ceremony. If this did not occur, the killer became an enemy and a blood feud began. The Indians did not recognize the battlefield as a distinct cultural zone in which killing was sanctioned to the exclusion of other acts of killing which were defined as murder. Europeans believed that murder was a crime which required blood revenge; the Indians believed that killings by enemies demanded such revenge whether in or out of battle. These views obviously complicated each culture's understanding of the military values of the other.

tal ideals relating to warfare. First, they saw the ideal warrior as brave and unflinching in the face of danger. A warrior should also be honest and generous, qualities demanded of him in peacetime as well as wartime. Undoubtedly, not every warrior was able to live up to these ideals all the time, but social pressures and expectations made young Indian men strive to achieve them. And they experienced real shame or even became social outcasts when they could not.

Another common attribute of intertribal warfare, as well as Native American warfare in general, was that Indian fighters were usually highly disciplined, well trained, and led by strong, competent, humane commanders. "In contrast to European armies," Armstrong Starkey points out,

> Indian discipline was founded on individual honor rather than corporal punishment; leaders were chosen according to merit based on courage and experience instead of privilege or purchase. Commanders were concerned to save their men's lives and believed that victory did not justify unnecessary sacrifice. There was no disgrace in retreating to await a more favorable occasion for battle. Indian leaders taught their men to move in scattered order and take advantage of the ground, to surround the enemy or avoid being surrounded. They practiced running and marksmanship and they became accustomed to endure hunger and hardship with patience and fortitude. While avoiding unnecessary casualties, the Indians were a martial people, ready to sell their lives dearly in defense of their homes.[39]

Tactics of Indian Armies

Although all, or at least most, North American Indian warriors were brave, disciplined, and well led, they did not all fight in the

An engraving shows a Florida chief, Holata Outina (standing, upper left), leading his army against another tribe with the help of French troops.

same manner. The tactics they employed in combat varied from region to region, partly because of the peculiarities of local terrains and climates but also because of differing social and cultural traditions dating back into the dim past. With rare exceptions, large-scale armies divided into distinct formations and executing formal battlefield tactics, an approach widely practiced in Europe, was unknown in native North America. Among the exceptions were the Aztec, Iroquois, and some Florida tribes, including the Calusa, Timucua, and Apalachee, who fielded hundreds and on occasion a few thousand warriors at one time.

It is questionable, however, how many of the troops in these armies actually partici-

pated in combat. In Florida, for example, the tactic of amassing a large army seems to have been intended mainly for show, probably to intimidate or frighten the enemy, since only a minority of the warriors fought one another. In 1564, a French observer described a war expedition by a local chief named Holata Outina:

He used to march with regular ranks, like an organized army; himself marching alone in the middle of the whole force, painted red. On the wings, or horns, of his order of march were his young men, the swiftest of whom, also painted red, acted as advanced guards and scouts for reconnoitering [scouting and gathering information about] the enemy. . . . They have heralds, who by cries of certain sorts direct when to halt, or to advance, or to attack, or to perform any other military duty. . . . After encamping, they are arranged in squads of ten each, the bravest men being put in squads by themselves. . . . The quartermasters place ten of these squads of the bravest men in a circle around [Outina]. About ten paces outside of this circle is placed another line of twenty squads; at twenty yards farther, another of forty squads; and so on, increasing the number and distance of these lines, according to the size of the army.[40]

Once these squads of warriors had been assembled, and similar squads had formed in the enemy's ranks (as the two armies faced each other across an open field), the attempted intimidation began. Groups of warriors from one army would shout insults at their opponents or step forward, brandish their weapons, and scream high-pitched war cries; members of the enemy army would do the same. This would go on sometimes for hours. Meanwhile, small bands of selected warriors from each army would slip away, hopefully unnoticed, and attack small groups of troops on the fringes of the enemy army. After these minor skirmishes, which typically resulted in few casualties, the armies retired and the battle was over.

More Common Tactics

Much more often, though, the number of warriors involved in intertribal conflicts was

relatively small—usually no more than a few dozen, and on occasion a few hundred, at a time. Not counting the atypical large-scale tactics employed by the Florida Indians, there were four main forms of attack in use across the continent, with numerous variations from place to place. In the plains and other relatively open, nonforested areas, a common approach was for opposing warriors to line up opposite each other and fire atlatls or arrows back and forth. Because shields were used by both sides, casualties were usually very light, and after a while the opposing forces would go home, feeling satisfied that they had vented their anger.

When the grievances that had led to fighting were more serious, a second, more lethal mode of combat might occur. According to Colin Taylor,

> The war chief led the whole line in a charge; often, this was preceded by the singing of a war song, the charge itself being initiated by a war cry. Hand-to-hand fighting then took place, the main weapon being a stone-headed war club. The outcome was generally brief and bloody. Territory was thus gained, together with loot, trophies, and scalps.[41]

Another kind of combat tactic, best described as guerrilla-type warfare, was common in the woodland areas of the East and the mountainous areas of the Southwest, especially after the introduction of the gun. Typically, warriors spread out and took advantage of trees, rocks, and other forms of cover. Discipline and coordination were still in effect, as the warriors made sure to support one another, each watching his companions' backs and providing covering fire for their movements. In Taylor's words,

> Woodland military tactics . . . maintained no regular formation; the warriors kept close enough together to support one another and, when hard pressed, retreated to the nearest available patch of woods where this style of warfare could be used to best advantage. Further, the shield and body armor, effective against the arrow and spear in earlier days, but no longer a protection against the penetrating power of the bullet . . . were largely abandoned.[42]

A fourth kind of tactic, one practiced often in intertribal wars across the continent, was raiding enemy villages and camps. According to the Piegan warrior Saukamappee, "The great mischief of war . . . [was] attacking and destroying small camps of ten to thirty tents."[43] Most often, raids were conducted before dawn because darkness helped hide the attackers and thereby ensure the advantage of

A nineteenth-century engraving depicts Native American warriors preparing to ambush the farm of a white settler. Guerrilla-style tactics were common in the eastern woodlands.

"MOURNING" WARFARE

One of the main tactics used by many Native American tribes in intertribal warfare, the revenge raid, was usually a part of what became known as "mourning" warfare. As explained here by Cherokee historian Tom Holm (in an article in the Encyclopedia of North American Indians*), this highly ritualized form of blood vengeance was driven by deep feelings of kinship and spirituality.*

When a kinsman or kinswoman died or was killed in battle, some groups believed, the clan's, tribe's, or nation's collective spiritual power was diminished directly in proportion to that of the slain person. Retaliatory raiding took place to take captives and/or kill a certain number of enemy warriors. In numerous cases, captives were adopted as replacements for deceased relatives. Killing an enemy or torturing a captive to death was intended to repair the metaphysical imbalance caused by a death. Some native American women literally "dried their tears" with the scalps of enemies killed in battle. All in all, mourning warfare kept populations relatively stable, promoted group cohesion, and reaffirmed the tribal sense of superiority.

surprise. The Tlingit and other tribes of the northwestern coasts particularly favored dawn raids in which they entered enemy dwellings, killed quickly, and then slipped away before the rest of the villagers could organize a defense.

A successful raid brought the attacking tribe more than just pride and prestige. It also helped support a complex of social customs within the tribe, most involving material rewards, especially after the infusion of horses, guns, and other commodities introduced by whites. Raiding, Holm writes,

added to tribal wealth. Apaches, Comanches, Kiowas, and numerous other tribes raided for foodstuffs, material goods, and, later, livestock. But there was another meaning placed on raiding; in addition to the simple acquisition of property, raiding was a means of gaining social rewards for the individual raider or that person's family. Consider the potlatches [ceremonial feasts] of northwest coast tribes, for example. Often the family or clan offering these formal displays of generosity obtained the goods they gave as gifts during the potlatches by raiding other tribes. Similarly, Kiowas [who lived on the plains] placed a great deal of emphasis on stealing horses. Those warriors who had acquired a number of horses often gave them away to less fortunate younger men. The recipients, in turn, could take part in mounted raids on enemy tribes for more horses. They could then pay back their benefactors and become benefactors themselves. In a like manner, when Cherokee warriors returned from a successful war they gave the booty they had collected to their female relatives for redistribution among those women who had no

This photo, taken about 1895, shows a group of northwestern warriors wearing ritualistic outfits, including masks intended to frighten and intimidate an enemy.

close male relatives who could participate in raids.[44]

Rituals of Warfare

What happened when a raiding party lost
the advantage of surprise and could not
carry through with its planned assault? Simply to retreat and go home was not a viable
option in most cases, since the failed warriors would be seen by their own people as
disgraceful cowards. One way around this
was to substitute a war ritual for actual combat. If a Tlingit raid was foiled, for example,
the warriors proceeded to put on a display
of intimidation similar to that of the Florida

Indian armies. The Tlingit warriors jumped
into canoes and rowed to a point within
shouting distance of the enemy village;
meanwhile, the enemy warriors gathered on
the beach. Then a Tlingit shaman (a holy
man who summoned the powers of gods
and spirits) stood up in his canoe and began
singing chants designed to belittle, threaten,
and frighten those on the beach. As Norman
Bancroft-Hunt tells it,

> Slowly [the shaman's] voice grew
> stronger as the spirits responded and
> then, with wild gesticulations [physi-
> cal gestures] and many curses . . . he
> began to harangue the people on the

beach, telling what spirits assisted him and how they would eat the hearts of the villagers, peck out their eyes, and tear out their tongues. Of how the serpent would twist their necks so they faced backwards, transform their women and children to stone, and leave their bones scattered over the beaches. [45]

After the Tlingit shaman was finished, the enemy shaman stepped forward and delivered his own barrage of curses and threats. Such verbal exchanges might go on for hours before the participants were satisfied that they had sufficiently vented their fury.

On the plains, in contrast, warfare rituals reached a high level in the coup, which came from a French word meaning "blow." (The Indians adopted it from French trappers in the Great Lakes region.) At first, a coup consisted of touching the body of an enemy warrior with a special stick, an act that demonstrated one's bravery and prestige. Later, a coup

This Plains Indian holds a coup stick. Each feather commemorates his successful accomplishment of a bold war deed.

sometimes took on the more general meaning of any bold war deed. Fighters often recited lists of their coups to fellow warriors and other members of the tribe; the more coups one had accumulated, the larger one's prestige and higher his status. In many tribes, accomplishing a certain number of coups granted a warrior the right to become a high war leader. A number of tribes awarded warriors an eagle's feather for each coup, a custom that resulted in the elaborate feather headdresses sported by the more experienced Plains fighters. Each tribe had its own preferences for and ranking of coups. "Among the Blackfeet," Farb explains,

> stealing an enemy's weapons was looked upon as the highest exploit. Among some other tribes, the bravest deed was to touch an enemy without hurting him. The least important exploit usually was killing an enemy, but even that deed was ranked according to the way it was done and the weapons that were used. The whole business of counting coups often became extremely involved. Among the Cheyenne, for example, coups could be counted by several warriors on a single enemy, but the coups were ranked in the strict order in which the

enemy was touched by the participants; it was immaterial who actually killed or wounded him.[46]

Other warfare rituals and ceremonies involved beliefs about death and the spirit world. Common was the idea that, under certain conditions, artisans could endow the weapons they crafted with magical powers. Some tribes held that warriors who had been in contact with an enemy were spiritually contaminated; upon returning home, they had to cleanse themselves through rituals such as fasting, vomiting, and abstaining from sex. Some Plains tribes took part in the so-called Sun Dance ceremony, in which young warriors tested their courage and endurance. At the climax of the ceremony, a young man allowed his breast to be pierced and a stick to be inserted into the wound; ropes were attached to the stick and also to the central pole of a lodge; the warrior then tried to tear himself free until he fainted from the searing pain.[47] During this initiation, the young man usually had a supernatural vision that enhanced his connection with the spirit world. These are only some of the ways in which war and its attendant rituals pervaded all levels of Native American life.

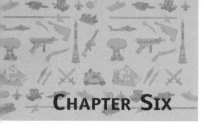

CHAPTER SIX

The Struggle Between Indians and Whites

Traditional fighting among Native American tribes had gone on for untold numbers of centuries. Yet the threats, feuds, battles, raids, and deaths that occurred over time had been small-scale and localized, and the overall toll and outcome of war was never catastrophic. Most tribes remained intact, and the general fabric of Indian society and life was not disrupted.

In contrast, the toll and ultimate outcome of warfare between Indians and whites was catastrophic. In a little more than two centuries, white civilization decimated the Native American tribes, destroying some and consigning the shattered remains of the others to poverty on reservations. This naturally raises the question of why the weapons and tactics that Indians had used effectively against one another were so much less effective against whites. To understand why the often heroic efforts of Native Americans to preserve their way of life ultimately failed, one must first consider how they waged war against whites; how Indians exploited their own traditional weapons and

tactics; and most important, how they tried to counter the whites' weapons and peculiar ideas about war.

Lying Gut-Eating Skunks

Among the white ideas that Indians found perplexing was the unusual formality and seeming foolishness of some of the battle tactics white soldiers had brought with them from Europe. These tactics were employed in a majority of battles during the American Revolution and continued in use in the next conflict with Britain, the War of 1812. During the latter war, the famous Sauk chief Black Hawk witnessed some of the fighting between Americans and British. He was astounded to see long lines of soldiers marching at each other in the open, completely vulnerable to volleys of musket and cannon fire. He later commented,

> Instead of stealing upon each other and taking every advantage to kill the enemy and save their own people . . . they march out, in open daylight,

71

Some Native Americans were perplexed at seeing white soldiers marching and firing at one another in the open. Many battles of the American Revolution were fought this way.

and fight, regardless of the number of warriors they may lose! After the battle is over, they retire to feast, and drink wine, as if nothing happened; after which, they make a statement in writing, of what they have done—each party claiming the victory![48]

This approach to fighting contrasted sharply with most Indian tactics, especially the guerrilla-style tactics typically employed by Indians east of the Mississippi. Throughout the 1700s, most whites saw such tactics as cowardly and barbaric and condemned Indians for using them (although some whites used them as well when they felt the situation warranted it). "Tensions between principle and practice

existed in the eighteenth century," Armstrong Starkey points out.

Indian warriors were not bound by European codes and conventions and it should not be surprising that they followed the imperatives of military necessity, which many soldiers believe to be the true law of war. Their "skulking way of war" involved many practices that Europeans thought were unfair or inhumane: ambushes, surprises, attacks on civilians, and cruel treatment of prisoners. Aimed fire was a controversial issue in itself. Indian sharpshooters had no scruples about aiming at sentries and officers, a practice often frowned upon by European regulars, who regarded it as tantamount to murder. . . . Ironically the Indians' mastery of European firearms confirmed their barbarian status in the eyes of their opponents.[49]

This clash of ideas on what constituted "civilized" warfare only reinforced the view of most whites that Indians were savages. Therefore, the argument went, whites were justified in killing Indians and taking their lands. Typical was this disparaging description of Indians printed in a white newspaper:

A set of miserable, dirty, lousy, blanketed, thieving, lying, sneaking, murdering, graceless, faithless, gut-eating skunks as the Lord ever permitted to infect the earth, and whose immediate and final extermination all men, except Indian agents and traders, should pray for.[50]

"Outnumbered as Well as Outarmed"

Thus, deep-seated hatred or contempt for Indians as a race became a dangerous factor that Native Americans had to contend with in their conflicts with whites, one that had not existed in intertribal warfare. Had the whites, like the Indians, lacked advanced technology, an industrial base, and a ready ability to make gunpowder, this factor may not have mattered so much. In such a scenario, at least the two sides might have met each other on more or less equal footing from a material standpoint. But the reality was that whites did have these advantages. And this enabled them to translate their In-

dian hatred into a systematic decimation of the natives.

The whites also had another advantage that the Indians found impossible to overcome in the long run—superior numbers. By 1820, the United States had a population of approximately 10 million, as compared to probably fewer than 500,000 Indians living in and west of the Ohio Valley. As time went on, of course, the disparity between these figures became ever larger. Also, the country's army grew steadily larger and better organized; there were more soldiers, more horses and wagons to carry them (as well as the system of railroads that expanded westward during the nineteenth century), and better communications, including the telegraph. As scholar Peter Nabokov puts it,

Neither stealthy ambushes nor full-scale assaults [by Indians] could stem the unending stream of white reinforcements. In the end, the Indian was simply outnumbered as well as outarmed. Warfare against the whites was at best only a holding action. Native fighting prowess was judged finally by how long a tribe could prolong its retreat or delay its surrender.[51]

Organized Brutality and Cruelty

The anti-Indian hostility, superior firepower, and greater numbers possessed by the whites were not the only debilitating factors that Native Americans had to deal with in their battles against whites. War atrocities were another. Hatred and fear of Indians, combined with strong feelings of superiority, gave many whites what they viewed as a

INCREASING WHITE FIREPOWER

As the nineteenth century wore on, the whites continued to widen the firepower gap between themselves and the Indians. In addition to rifles and other handheld guns, the whites developed the Gatling gun, which had a cluster of ten barrels. A soldier turned the cluster with a crank, discharging the barrels in succession. In theory, the weapon could fire four hundred rounds per minute; however, because of certain mechanical drawbacks, it rarely performed this well. Nevertheless, army units equipped with Gatling guns had a clear advantage over the Indians they encountered. The same can be said for the army's primary artillery piece: a twelve-pound howitzer that could fire two shells per minute, each with an effective range of well over nine hundred yards. Like the muskets used in the past, the howitzers were effective not so much because of the casualties they inflicted but because of their novelty. The big guns often frightened and drove off attacks by Native Americans who were unfamiliar with such weapons.

The advantage in firepower held by whites over Indians in the nineteenth century is well illustrated by the Gatling gun, pictured here.

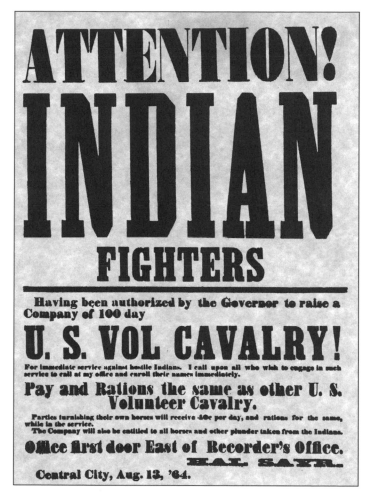

ATTENTION!
INDIAN
FIGHTERS

Having been authorized by the Governor to raise a Company of 100 day

U. S. VOL CAVALRY!

For immediate service against hostile Indians. I call upon all who wish to engage in such service to call at my office and enroll their names immediately.

Pay and Rations the same as other U. S. Volunteer Cavalry.

Parties furnishing their own horses will receive 40c per day, and rations for the same, while in the service.
The Company will also be entitled to all horses and other plunder taken from the Indians.

Office first door East of Recorder's Office.
HAL. SAYR.

Central City, Aug. 13, '64.

An 1860s recruitment poster urges whites to join the fight against the Comanche in Colorado. Some of these recruits took part in the Sand Creek massacre.

sort of license to attack poorly armed or even unarmed Indian bands. Sometimes such massacres occurred even after a group of Indians had signaled its desire to stop fighting and make peace. The whites who took part in such atrocities displayed a level of savagery that matched or surpassed the worst cruelties that had occurred in inter-tribal warfare. Tom Holm describes two notorious incidents of this sort:

> On November 29, 1864, Colonel John M. Chivington led his Third Colorado Cavalry Regiment in an attack on a Cheyenne and Arapaho camp at Sand Creek, a tributary of the Arkansas River in southeastern Colorado. Black Kettle, the Cheyenne leader, had just concluded negotiations on a new peace treaty when Chivington's men attacked. Two hundred Cheyennes died in the onslaught, but, what was worse, Chivington's men dismembered Cheyenne corpses and brought hundreds of body parts back to Denver to be put on display at the local

75

theater. Attacks on tribes by civilian ir-
regulars, however, were even more
horrible than those made by regular
army troops. In 1871 at Camp Grant,
Arizona, for example, a Tucson citizens' group killed and scalped most of
the Apache males in the camp, and
then raped, murdered, and scalped the
women. They took the children to be
sold into slavery.[52]

These awful events occurred in the western frontier near the end of the great conflict
between Indians and whites for control of
the continent. However, such organized brutality and cruelty by whites, sometimes
verging on out-and-out genocide (the systematic destruction of an entire race or
group of people), was neither new nor con-
fined to the West. Well before the United
States had been established, various European groups who were in the process of settling the eastern coastal regions sought to
exterminate bands or even whole tribes of
Native Americans. Often, there was no need
to resort to large-scale attacks and massacres
like those at Sand Creek and Camp Grant.
Instead, white leaders instituted policies that
provided economic incentives for individuals, bounty hunters as well as ordinary pri-
vate citizens, to go out and murder Indians.
According to Peter Farb,

White settlers early offered to pay
bounties on dead Indians, and scalps
were actual proof of the deed. Governor Kieft of [the Dutch colony of]
New Netherland is usually credited
with originating the idea of paying for
Indian scalps, as they were more con-
venient to handle than whole heads,

and they offered the same proof that
an Indian had been killed. By liberal
payments for scalps, the Dutch virtually cleared southern New York and
New Jersey of Indians before the English supplanted them. By 1703 the
colony of Massachusetts was paying
the equivalent of $60 for every Indian
scalp. In the mid– eighteenth century,
Pennsylvania fixed the bounty for a
male Indian scalp at $134; a female's
was worth only $50. Some White en-
trepreneurs simply hatcheted [to
death] any old Indians that still survived in their towns. The French also
used scalp-taking as an instrument of
geopolitics. In the competition over
the Canadian fur trade, they offered
the Micmac Indians a bounty for
every scalp they took from the
Beothuk of Newfoundland. By 1827
an expedition to Newfoundland failed
to find a single survivor of this once
numerous and proud people.[53]

This insidious approach to warfare was completely alien to Native Americans, and the
fact that they did not expect and could not
prepare for it left them fatally vulnerable.

Removal and Relocation
Just as devastating to many Indian tribes
were the white tactics of removing Indians
from their ancestral lands, by force if necessary, and relocating them in unfamiliar, less
productive lands farther west. By 1820, the
United States had defeated or destroyed
most of the Native American tribes east of
the Mississippi River and whites had taken
over much Indian land. However, more than
120,000 Indians still lived in the region. In

An eighteenth-century engraving depicts whites slaughtering Indian women. Some eastern municipalities offered bounties for men who would kill Indians and collect their scalps.

particular, the Cherokee, Creek, Choctaw, Chickasaw, and Seminole tribes still occupied a great deal of fertile, valuable territory in the Southeast. Meanwhile, white settlers continued to flood over the Appalachian Mountains in search of new lands. They not only wanted the remaining Indian lands for themselves, they also did not want Indians living near them.

To appease the settlers, as well as to expand U.S. borders and national interests, the government eventually developed plans to remove the eastern Indians from their lands and ship them west. The chief architect of the policy, Andrew Jackson (who

served as president from 1829 to 1837), had grown up on the Tennessee frontier. He had lived near Indians and fought them on several occasions, and he saw them as both uncivilized and dangerous. In 1830, Jackson pushed the Indian Removal Act through Congress. Though the law did not specifically mention the use of force, it was clear to all that any Indians who refused to move would be left to the mercy of their hostile white neighbors.

Put simply, Jackson's removal policy proceeded with cold efficiency. Eastern Indians had to move west of the Mississippi to a special region that the whites called

JACKSON DEMANDS THAT THE CHEROKEE LEAVE

The following is part of the letter (quoted in John Ehle's Trail of Tears*) made public on April 7, 1835, by President Andrew Jackson in which he delivered an ultimatum to the Cherokee in Georgia to vacate their lands.*

My Friends: I have long viewed your condition with great interest. For many years I have been acquainted with your people. . . . Listen to me . . . as your fathers have listened, while I communicate to you my sentiments on the critical state of your affairs. . . . Most of your young people are uneducated, and are liable to be brought into collision at all times with their white neighbors. Your young men are acquiring habits of intoxication [drunkenness]. . . . The [wild] game has disappeared among you and you must depend upon agriculture and the mechanical arts for support. And yet, a large portion of your people have acquired little or no property in the soil itself, or in any article of personal property which can be useful to them. How, under these circumstances, can you live in the country you now occupy? Your condition must become worse and worse, and you will ultimately disappear, as so many tribes have done before you. . . . All of this I warned your people when I met them in council eighteen years ago. I then advised them to sell out their possessions east of the Mississippi and to remove to the country west of that river. This advice I have continued to give you. . . . Circumstances that cannot be controlled, and which are beyond the reach of human laws, render it impossible that you can flourish in the midst of a civilized community. You have but one remedy within your reach. And that is, to remove to the west and join your countrymen, who are already established there. And the sooner you do this, the sooner you will commence your career of improvement and prosperity. . . . The choice is now before you. May the Great Spirit teach you how to choose. The fate of your women and children, the fate of your people to the remotest generation, depend upon this issue.

Robert Lindreaux's famous painting of the terrible Trail of Tears. More than four thousand Cherokee died in the long march west.

"Indian Country," encompassing large parts of what are now Oklahoma, Kansas, and Nebraska. Yet many Indians bravely resisted removal. The Seminole in Florida put up a bitter fight, for example, two thousand of them managing to escape into some large swamps. (The army spent years trying to root them out and finally gave up and allowed a few Seminole to remain in Florida.)

The Cherokee living in Georgia also refused to move. So President Jackson's successor, Martin Van Buren, ordered seven thousand troops to remove them by force. The soldiers dragged some seventeen thousand Cherokee from their homes, after which gangs of whites looted the houses and burned them to the ground. Guarding the Indians closely, the soldiers drove them in a forced march westward, an ordeal that became known as the "Trail of Tears." Each day, dozens of Cherokee died of starvation, exposure to freezing temperatures, or sickness. A white witness later recalled,

> Many of the aged Indians were suffering extremely from the fatigue of the journey. . . . Several were then quite ill. . . . The sick and the feeble were carried in wagons. . . . Even aged females, apparently nearly ready to drop into the grave, were traveling with heavy burdens attached to the back—on the sometimes frozen ground, and sometimes muddy streets, with no covering for the feet except what nature had given them. . . . They buried fourteen or fifteen [Cherokee] at every stopping place. [54]

In all, more than four thousand Cherokee died before the tribe reached its destination in Indian Country in 1839.

By the early 1840s, more than sixty thousand Indians had been removed from the eastern United States, and about fifteen thousand of these, or about one-quarter, had died on the way west. The survivors hoped that things would get better once they reached Indian Country. But many discovered instead that their troubles had only begun. Forcing so many tribes with different cultures and customs to live close together in the same area was a recipe for trouble; many western tribes saw relocated eastern tribes as intruders. Disputes broke out over hunting rights and other matters, disagreements that often led to new rounds of intertribal warfare.

Some Indians Continue to Resist

The intertribal wars spawned by U.S. removal and relocation efforts served only to weaken a native culture that was already lacking in unity, coordination, numbers, firepower, and advanced weapons technology. When Indians fought Indians, none of these factors was either applicable or decisive, but when Indians fought whites, especially from 1850 on, all of these factors worked together to make the collapse of Native American resistance inevitable.

At the time, however, most western Indians did not see their own demise as inevitable. A common belief among many of them was that if they were brave enough, fought hard enough, and won the support of their gods and spirits, they could somehow stop the white advance. This belief may seem hopelessly naïve now. But it is understandable, since the alternative—the utter destruction of the natives' way of life—was simply unthinkable.

Plains warriors attack a white wagon train, hoping to halt the westward advance of white civilization.

Thus, despite the whites' formidable advantages, in the last few decades of the nineteenth century many Indian tribes stepped up their resistance against white settlers and soldiers. War parties of Sioux, Cheyenne, Arapaho, and other tribes regularly raided white outposts and wagon trains in an effort to slow the encroachment of whites onto Indian lands. In response, the U.S. Army mounted one campaign after another against them. In the late 1860s and into the 1870s, numerous skirmishes, battles, and mas-sacres took place on the plains as the Kiowa, Comanche, Sioux, and others desperately struggled to protect their hunting grounds and way of life.

Only on rare occasions were these efforts successful. And in the long run, the few Indian victories had no decisive or lasting effect on the overall conflict between Indians and whites. Usually these Indian victories resulted from a combination of two general factors: boldness, courage, and a highly efficient use of weapons and tactics by Native

Americans, and a corresponding inefficient use of weapons and tactics by U.S. commanders. The result in these few cases was that Indians were able to blunt or nullify the whites' clearly superior logistics and firepower.

Unquestionably, the most celebrated example was the defeat of George Armstrong Custer and the Seventh Cavalry near the Little Bighorn River in southern Montana in 1876. Custer was trying to destroy a temporary alliance of several Plains tribes who had come together in one large encampment near the river. After dividing his forces in an attempt to attack the camp from several angles, his own contingent

was surrounded and wiped out by warriors led by Crazy Horse and other chiefs.

Over the years, the story of the battle has been retold, reconstructed, and depicted almost endlessly in books and movies. But the actual details of the event are still disputed, partly because none of Custer's 267 men survived to tell the tale. A recently discovered narrative by a soldier serving in an army unit that fought on another side of the Indian camp is fascinating and valuable for its insights into Custer's overall campaign. But the author did not actually witness the Seventh Cavalry's demise.[55] Several accounts said to be by Indians who fought in or observed

A LESSER KNOWN INDIAN VICTORY

When people think about Indian battles, especially Indian victories, they usually recall the defeat of George Custer by the Sioux and their allies at the Little Bighorn on June 25, 1876. Few people today realize that the Sioux delivered U.S. troops another major defeat about a week before at Rosebud Creek, a few miles east of the Little Bighorn. Reuben B. Davenport, an American journalist who fought in the battle, later published an eyewitness account, briefly excerpted here (from Jerome Greene's Battles and Skirmishes of the Great Sioux War*).*

The two battalions of the Third Cavalry were resting on the south side of the creek and the one of the Second [Cavalry] on the north side. Suddenly yells were heard beyond the low hill on the north, and shots were fired. . . . The cavalry were making ready to mount, when [the soldiers' Indian] scouts came galloping back . . . hallooing that the

Sioux were charging. . . . Seeing the long gallant skirmish line [of soldiers] pause, however, they [the Sioux] dashed forward on the right and left, and in an instant nearly every point of vantage within, in front and in the rear, and on the flank of the line was covered with savages wildly circling their ponies and charging hither and thither, while they fired from their seats with wonderful rapidity and accuracy. . . . The suspense grew terrible as the [soldiers'] position was every moment more perilous as the Sioux appeared at intervals on the left flank, charging on their ponies and each time further toward the rear. . . . [The white commander ordered his men to retreat.] Looking behind, I saw a dozen Sioux surrounding a group of soldiers who had straggled behind the retreat. Six were killed at one spot. . . . The Sioux rode so close to their victims that they shot them in the face with revolvers and the powder blackened the flesh.

the battle survived orally and were later written down in English. Although some of these accounts are vague or contradictory, a number of others support reconstructions by military historians and are likely accurate. According to a Cheyenne chief, Brave Wolf, "It was hard fighting; very hard all the time. I have been in many hard fights, but never saw such brave men."[56] Crow King, a Sioux, concurred in his own account, which maintains that when Custer's men found themselves surrounded, they dismounted and fought on foot:

> They tried to hold onto their horses, but as we pressed closer they let go their horses. We crowded them toward our main camp and killed them all. They kept in order and fought like

brave warriors as long as they had a man left.[57]

Though stunning and memorable, this great Indian victory was an unusual exception in the ongoing struggle between Indians and whites. It resulted mainly from the fact that Custer unwisely divided his forces, so his own unit was greatly outnumbered. Also, the large encampment of Indians he encountered was itself highly unusual; never before or after this incident did so many Indian warriors come together in one place to fight against the white onslaught. Moreover, after the battle, the flood of white settlers and soldiers became larger than ever. And the conquest and exploitation of Indians and Indian lands continued unabated.

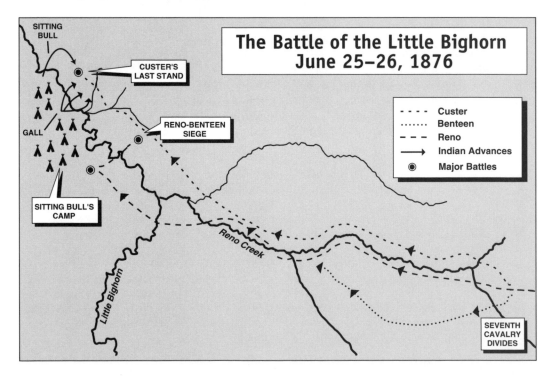

SITTING BULL

CUSTER'S LAST STAND

GALL

RENO-BENTEEN SIEGE

SITTING BULL'S CAMP

The Battle of the Little Bighorn June 25–26, 1876

- - - - Custer
.... Benteen
- - - Reno
→ Indian Advances
◉ Major Battles

Reno Creek

Little Bighorn

SEVENTH CAVALRY DIVIDES

In this scene from Little Big Man, *one of many films that have restaged the Little Bighorn battle, Indian forces race downhill toward Custer's troops.*

Near the close of the nineteenth century, the scattered remnants of Native American civilization in the American West turned to one last weapon. Perplexed, frustrated, and desperate, they hoped it would suddenly and ferociously aid them in their plight and restore the natural balance the whites had so violently torn asunder. The problem was that this particular weapon—unlike clubs, knives, tomahawks, guns, and forced relocation—could not be swung, fired, held, or even seen. One of the strangest and saddest chapters in the history of warfare was about to begin.

Faith as a Weapon: The Ghost Dance

Despite generations of brave warriors and their great skill with weapons, both traditional ones and those borrowed from the whites, Native Americans were unable to stem the tide of white settlers and soldiers across the continent. By the late 1880s, all tribes east of the Mississippi and most of those west of it had been defeated or had given up the fight. Many Indians now lived in abject poverty on reservations. And in some places the whites had begun a systematic policy of assimilation, with the goal of convincing and teaching Indians to think and act like whites. Over time, architects of the policy hoped, the Indians would be absorbed into white society. And in time, there would no longer be an Indian "problem" since there would no longer be any Indians. No attempt was made to disguise or apologize for the project's stated goals, which were clearly racist. One white official freely admitted that the objective was to "kill the Indian, spare the man," so the policy of assimilation was, in effect, "a great pulverizing engine for breaking up the tribal mass."[58]

Faced with what amounted to eventual extermination as a people, a number of Native Americans resorted to desperate measures. In a last-gasp attempt to resist the whites and keep their own cultural traditions intact, they turned to a highly unconventional weapon. It consisted of an unusual new religious belief that promised the salvation of their race. Called the Ghost Dance, it became popular among western Indians, mainly on the Plains reservations, in 1890.

Mixing religion and war was nothing new for Indians. For centuries, Native Americans had called on their gods and the spirits of the dead to help them in battle; through visions and paintings on shields and weapons, they had invoked such supernatural aid. But the Ghost Dance was different. Instead of protecting an individual warrior or tribe in a particular battle, it purported to become a mighty umbrella of protection for all Indians, as well as an instrument of instant deliverance from white oppression. Through magical powers, leaders of the dance predicted, most whites would die and the Indians would push the rest eastward into the ocean. In reality, the Ghost Dance was nothing more than a hopeless dream born out of fear and desperation. And sadly, those who succumbed to its allure ended up either dead or crushed by disillusion and disappointment.

Origins of the Ghost Dance

The Ghost Dance that erupted on the Great Plains in 1890 was a larger and more developed offshoot of an earlier, more localized religious movement. In the late 1860s, the Union Pacific Railroad had completed its first transcontinental run. The trains passed through the lands of the Northern Paiute, who dwelled near the border of Nevada and California. Seeing these great "iron horses"

carrying passengers back and forth apparently inspired a local Paiute prophet named Wodziwob to envision a strange and miraculous event. A very big train would soon come, he said; on it would be his ancestors, along with those of any Paiute that believed in him; and all of the deceased would be living once more. Furthermore, there would be a huge explosion that would destroy all the whites in the area and miraculously leave behind their goods for the Indians to use. To make these things happen sooner, Wodziwob claimed, believers should dance around a ceremonial pole.

No train came bearing the resurrected dead. Nor were any whites killed in a magical explosion. So, Wodziwob was discredited and the local Indians abandoned the

A painting completed about 1900 shows a group of Arapaho men and women taking part in the Ghost Dance. It was a last, desperate attempt to save their way of life.

ceremonial dances he had instituted. However, this strange dream of deliverance did not die completely. Wodziwob had an assistant who still believed in it, and the assistant passed on the basic tenets of the belief to his own son, a young Paiute named Wovoka.

As Wovoka grew older and watched the onslaught of white civilization continue, he reformulated the idea of a miracle that would stop that onslaught. His vision, which was bolder and broader in scope than Wodzi-

wob's, was based not only on traditional Native American religious ideas but on concepts from Christianity. In particular, he was influenced by the Mormons, who had settled in nearby Utah and had extensive contacts with tribes in the region. It became part of Mormon belief, Peter Farb explains,

> that the Indians represented the remnants of the Hebrew tribes taken into captivity by the Assyrians some 2,500 years earlier. The Mormons sent emis-

Joseph Smith, founder of the Mormons, preaches to the Indians. His ideas strongly influenced the beliefs that led to the Ghost Dance.

saries to the Indians . . . inviting them to join the Mormon colonies and to be baptized. Joseph Smith [founder of the Mormons] was also supposed to have prophesied in 1843 that when he reached his eighty-fifth year—that is, in 1890—the Messiah [savior of humanity, pictured by Christians as Jesus Christ] would appear in human form. . . . The Mormons found it perfectly understandable that in the promised year the Messiah should appear first among the Indians rather than among whites, for the Indians were descendants of Jews and thus possessed priority.[59]

Wovoka took it on himself to fulfill the prophecy. In 1890, he stepped forward, claiming to be the Messiah, and initiated the Ghost Dance. He stated the basic precepts of the belief, while borrowing another biblical image—the great flood—saying,

All Indians must dance, everywhere, [and] keep on dancing. Pretty soon, in [the] next spring, [the] Great Spirit [will] come. He [will] bring back all game of every kind. The game [will] be thick everywhere. All dead Indians [will] come back and live again. They [will] all be strong, just like young men, [and] be young again. Old blind Indian[s] [will] see again and get young and have [a] fine time. When [the] Great Spirit comes this way, then all the Indians [will] go to [the] mountains, high up away from the whites. Whites can't hurt Indians then. Then, while [the] Indians [are] way up high, [a] big flood comes like water and all

white people [will] die, get drowned. After that, [the] water [will] go away and then nobody [will be left] but Indians everywhere and game [of] all kinds thick. Then [the] medicine man [must] tell Indians to send word to all Indians to keep up [their] dancing and the good time will come. Indians who don't dance, who don't believe in this word, will grow little, just about a foot high, and stay that way. Some of them will be turned into wood and be burned in fire.[60]

A Fantastic Vision Spreads

The Ghost Dance spread rapidly across the mountains, deserts, and plains. And thousands of downtrodden, desperate Indians joined its ranks. However, despite Wovoka's warning about what would happen to Indians who did not believe in the Ghost Dance, many western Indians refused to take part. Tribes in California and Oregon rejected it, perhaps because they remembered how Wodziwob's predictions had failed to come true. And the Navajo of Arizona and New Mexico declined to take part, probably because they had a deep fear of the dead and ghosts, and the new religion promised that the spirits of the dead would return to the earth.

Those tribes that did accept Wovoka as the Messiah rallied to unleash the new weapon of faith on the whites. Wovoka himself remained in Nevada, and delegates from various regions visited him and then carried his message to their respective tribes. Local interpretations and variations of the new religion were thus inevitable. Among these variations was that of a Sioux leader, Short Bull, who told his people:

In the Sioux version of the Ghost Dance, a special sacred shirt (like this one photographed in 1912) rendered the wearer immune to white men's bullets.

Now, there will be a tree sprout up and there all the members of our religion and the tribe just gather together. That will be the place where we will see our dead relations. But before this time, we must dance the balance of this moon [i.e., the rest of the month], at the end of which time the earth will shiver very hard [i.e., there will be a powerful earthquake]. Whenever this thing occurs, I will start the wind to blow. We are the ones who will then see our [dead] fathers, mothers, and everybody. We, the tribe of Indians, are the ones who are living a sacred life. God, our father himself, has told and commanded and shown me to do these things.[61]

Short Bull and some other interpreters of the Ghost Dance added various far-fetched ideas that had not been in Wovoka's original and already fantastic vision. For example, the Sioux and several other Plains tribes came to believe the claim that wearing special shirts during the faith's ceremonies would make Indians immune to white soldiers' bullets. "If the soldiers surround you four deep," Short Bull advised,

three of you, on whom I have put holy shirts, will sing a song, which I have taught you, around them, when some of them will drop dead. Then the rest will start to run, but their horses will sink into the earth. The riders will jump from their horses, but they will sink into the earth also. Then you can do as you desire with them. Now, you must know this, that all the soldiers and that race will be dead. There will be only five thousand of them left living on earth. My friends and relations, this is straight and true. [62]

A Dream Dies at Wounded Knee

Hearing reports of entire tribes swept up in the Ghost Dance, U.S. political and military leaders feared that the new religion would lead to dangerous uprisings both on and off the reservations. So soldiers began arresting Ghost Dance leaders. The climax of this campaign occurred in late December 1890 when U.S. cavalry units surrounded a group of Sioux, including a number of Ghost Dancers, along Wounded Knee Creek in South Dakota. During the attempt to arrest the Indians, someone—whether a soldier or an Indian is unknown—fired a weapon, initiating a killing spree. The soldiers fired repeatedly at unarmed men, women, and children. A few minutes later, 153 Indians, including the group's leader, Chief Big Foot, lay dead.

As it had in 1870 in Nevada, the Ghost Dance had once more proven a false and forlorn hope. And the strange new faith disappeared as quickly as it had materialized, one more broken weapon the Indians were forced to discard in their long and vain struggle against the whites. For as it turned out, the terrible incident at Wounded Knee was the last major battle of the Indian wars

Members of a U.S. Army unit collect the bodies of the 153 Sioux men, women, and children massacred at Wounded Knee. It was the last major armed incident in the Indian wars.

of North America. Later remembering that fateful encounter, Black Elk, a Sioux holy man, delivered a lament that might stand as an epitaph for all the generations of warriors who had fought to maintain a way of life now lost. "When I look back now," he said,

> I can still see the butchered women and children lying heaped and scattered all along the crooked gulch as plain as when I saw them with eyes still young. And I can see that something else died there in the bloody mud, and was buried in the blizzard. A people's dream died there. . . . There is no center any longer, and the sacred tree is dead.[63]

Notes

Introduction: Two Very Different Concepts of Warfare

1. Tom Holm, "Warriors and Warfare," in Frederick E. Hoxie, ed., *Encyclopedia of North American Indians.* Boston: Houghton Mifflin, 1996, p. 666.
2. Dale Van Every, *The Disinherited: The Lost Birthright of the American Indian.* New York: Morrow, 1976, p. 18.

Chapter One: Precontact Offensive Weapons

3. Robert M. Utley and Wilcomb E. Washburn, *Indian Wars.* Boston: Houghton Mifflin, 1977, p. 149.
4. Colin F. Taylor, *Native American Weapons.* Norman: University of Oklahoma Press, 2001, p. 15.
5. Taylor, *Native American Weapons,* p. 37.
6. Garcilaso De La Vega, *Florida of the Inca,* trans. John and Jeannette Varner. Houston: University of Texas Press, 1951, p. 597.
7. Zebulon Pike, *An Account of Expeditions to the Sources of the Mississippi, and Through the Western Parts of Louisiana.* Philadelphia: C. and A. Conrad, 1810, pp. 10–11.
8. Reginald Laubin, *American Indian Archery.* Norman: University of Oklahoma Press, 1991, p. 1.

9. Quoted in Marvin C. Ross, ed., *The West of Alfred Jacob Miller.* Norman: University of Oklahoma Press, 1968, p. 60.
10. Paul H. Carlson, *The Plains Indians.* College Station: Texas A&M University Press, 1998, p. 62.

Chapter Two: Weapons Borrowed from the Whites

11. Quoted in John C. Dann, ed., *The Revolution Remembered: Eyewitness Accounts of the War for Independence.* Chicago: University of Chicago Press, 1980, p. 275.
12. Quoted in Harold L. Peterson, *American Indian Tomahawks.* New York: Museum of the American Indian, 1971, p. 33.
13. Quoted in Taylor, *Native American Weapons,* p. 33.
14. Taylor, *Native American Weapons,* pp. 33–34.
15. Archer Jones, *The Art of War in the Western World.* New York: Oxford University Press, 1987, pp. 269–70.
16. Ian V. Hogg, *Armies of the American Revolution.* Englewood Cliffs, NJ: Prentice-Hall, 1975, p. 66.
17. Armstrong Starkey, *European and Native American Warfare, 1675–1815.* Norman: University of Oklahoma Press, 1998, pp. 21–22.

18. Laubin, *American Indian Archery,* p. 3.

Chapter Three: Defensive Weapons and Tactics

19. "Other foreigners" refers to the Japanese, who apparently made some sporadic contacts with the Eskimo in North America's northwestern sector.
20. Taylor, *Native American Weapons,* pp. 80–81.
21. Quoted in Taylor, *Native American Weapons,* p. 123.
22. Quoted in Elliott Coues, ed., *The History of the Lewis and Clark Expedition,* vol. 2. New York: Francis P. Harper, 1893, p. 561.
23. Quoted in Frank R. Secoy, *Changing Military Patterns of the Great Plains Indians.* Norman: University of Oklahoma Press, 1992, p. 35.
24. George Catlin, *Letters and Notes on the Manners, Customs, and Conditions of North American Indians,* vol. 1, 1844. Reprint: New York: Dover, 1973, p. 271.
25. Norman Bancroft-Hunt, *Warriors: Warfare and the Native American Indian.* London: Salamander Books, 1995, pp. 22–23.
26. Bancroft-Hunt, *Warriors,* p. 30.

Chapter Four: Horses Transform Warfare on the Plains

27. Carlson, *The Plains Indians,* p. 39.
28. Quoted in John Bakeless, *Eyes of Discovery.* New York: Dover, 1961, p. 92.
29. Carlson, *The Plains Indians,* p. 41.
30. Peter Farb, *Man's Rise to Civilization as Shown by the Indians of North America from Primeval Times to the Coming of the Industrial State.* New York: E.P. Dutton, 1968, p. 156.
31. Carlson, *The Plains Indians,* p. 53.
32. Carlson, *The Plains Indians,* p. 38.
33. Farb, *Man's Rise to Civilization,* p. 150.
34. Catlin, *Letters and Notes,* vol. 1, p. 321.
35. Farb, *Man's Rise to Civilization,* p. 167.

Chapter Five: When Indians Fought Indians

36. Holm, "Warriors and Warfare," pp. 666–67.
37. Utley and Washburn, *Indian Wars,* p. 149.
38. Farb, *Man's Rise to Civilization,* p. 160.
39. Starkey, *European and Native American Warfare,* p. 18.
40. Quoted in Emma L. Fundeburk, *Southeastern Indians: Life Portraits, 1564–1860.* Metuchen, NJ: Scarecrow, 1969, p. 99.
41. Taylor, *Native American Weapons,* pp. 88–89.
42. Taylor, *Native American Weapons,* pp. 92–93.
43. Quoted in Secoy, *Changing Military Patterns,* p. 35.
44. Holm, "Warriors and Warfare," p. 667.
45. Bancroft-Hunt, *Warriors,* p. 191.
46. Farb, *Man's Rise to Civilization,* pp. 156–57.
47. This ritual was faithfully depicted in the 1970 feature film *A Man Called Horse,* starring Richard Harris. The film is notable for its accurate portrayal of many customs of the Sioux people and is highly recommended for its educational as well as entertainment value.

Chapter Six: The Struggle Between Indians and Whites

48. Quoted in Peter Nabokov, ed., *Native American Testimony*. New York: Harper and Row, 1978, p. 93.

49. Starkey, *European and Native American Warfare*, pp. 26–27.

50. Quoted in R.F. Spencer and J.D. Jennings, *The Native Americans*. New York: Harper and Row, 1965, p. 498.

51. Nabokov, *Native American Testimony*, p. 95.

52. Tom Holm, "Wars: 1850–1900," p. 673.

53. Farb, *Man's Rise to Civilization*, p. 158.

54. Quoted in John Ehle, *Trail of Tears: The Rise and Fall of the Cherokee Nation*. New York: Doubleday, 1988, pp. 357–58.

55. See William O. Taylor, *With Custer on the Little Bighorn*. New York: Viking, 1996.

56. Quoted in Edgar I. Stewart, *Custer's Luck*. Norman: University of Oklahoma Press, 1955, p. 459.

57. Quoted in Dee Brown, *Bury My Heart at Wounded Knee: An Indian History of the American West*. New York: Holt, Rinehart and Winston, 1970, p. 296.

Epilogue: Faith as a Weapon: The Ghost Dance

58. Quoted in Ward Churchill, *A Little Matter of Genocide: Holocaust Denial in the Americas, 1492 to the Present*. San Francisco: City Lights Books, 1997, p. 245.

59. Farb, *Man's Rise to Civilization*, p. 334.

60. Quoted in Brown, *Bury My Heart at Wounded Knee*, p. 416.

61. Quoted in Stephen Longstreet, *War Cries on Horseback: The Story of the Indian Wars of the Great Plains*. New York: W.H. Allen, 1971, pp. 322–23.

62. Quoted in Longstreet, *War Cries on Horseback*, p. 323.

63. Quoted in Brown, *Bury My Heart at Wounded Knee*, p. 446.

Glossary

artillery: Cannons.

atlatl: A throwing stick consisting of a wooden handle attached to a wooden socket; the back of a spear was inserted into the socket. The user flipped the stick to release the spear.

blow tube (or blowgun): A hollow tube that emits a dart from one end when the user blows on the other end.

bore: The diameter of the inside of a gun's barrel.

breech: The back end of a gun's barrel.

coup: From a French word meaning "blow," a war ritual in which a warrior touched the body of an enemy warrior or performed some other brave deed to demonstrate his bravery and prestige.

flaking: A process of sharpening a stone blade by steadily chipping away small pieces.

flank: The side or wing of a military formation. To "outflank" the enemy is to move one's own troops around enemy flanks, exposing them to attack from the side and rear as well as the front.

flintlock: A mechanism for firing a gun in which a piece of flint strikes a piece of steel, producing a spark that ignites the gunpowder.

foot surround: A prehorse method of hunting bison in which hunter-warriors formed a circle around one or more animals, then tightened the circle and killed them with spears or arrows.

Ghost Dance: A religious movement that appeared suddenly in 1890. Centered in the Great Plains, its members believed that dancing would invoke the destruction of whites and bring deceased Indians back to life.

matchlock: A mechanism for firing a gun in which pulling the trigger brings a lighted match into contact with a small pan of gunpowder, which flashes and ignites the gunpowder inside the barrel.

musket (or firelock): An early gun with a smooth bore that fired by means of either a matchlock or flintlock mechanism.

muzzle: The front end of a gun's barrel.

palisade: A wall made of vertical timber poles planted deep in the ground and lashed together with strips of rawhide or rope.

percussion cap: A device for firing a gun. When the operator pulls the trigger, a metal hammer strikes a metal plate coated with a chemical, which ignites, firing the weapon.

pipe tomahawk: A hatchet whose head has a blade on one side and a pipe bowl on the other so that it can be used as either a weapon or a peace pipe.

precontact: The state of North American Indian culture, or any given tribe, before making the first contact with white civilization.

ramrod: A stick used by early gunmen to push the powder and ball down into the gun barrel.

rifle: A gun with a rifled bore, or a barrel that has a set of spiral grooves etched on its inside.

self (or simple) bow: A bow made from a single piece of wood.

sinew: Animal tendon.

smoothbore: A firearm, such as the musket, that has a barrel with a smooth inside surface.

windage: In firearms, the space between the edge of the ball (or bullet) and the inside of the barrel.

For Further Reading

Joseph Bruchac, *The Trail of Tears.* New York: Random House, 1999. A very well-written, moving book describing the U.S. government's terrible removal of the Cherokee Indians from Georgia.

Stan Hoig, *The Cheyenne.* New York: Chelsea House, 1990. This is a worthwhile introduction to one of the most famous of the western Plains tribes, which was defeated by the U.S. Army in the nineteenth century.

Stuart A. Kallen and Deanne Durrett, *Native American Chiefs and Warriors.* San Diego: Lucent Books, 1999. Part of Lucent's History Makers series, this book is loaded with valuable information about some of the more important Native American leaders during the American Indian wars.

Allison Lassieur, *Before the Storm: American Indians Before the Europeans.* New York: Facts On File, 1998. An informative, fascinating examination of Indian life and customs on the eve of European colonization. The author includes some excellent material gathered by modern archaeologists.

Catherine J. Long, *The Cherokee.* San Diego: Lucent Books, 2000. A fine overview of the background, struggles, and customs of the tribe that endured the deprivations of Indian removal, including the infamous "Trail of Tears."

Bill McAuliffe and Lucile Davis, *Chief Joseph of the Nez Percé: A Photo-Illustrated Biography.* Mankato, MN: Bridgestone Books, 1997. A colorful look at the great chief who bravely tried to resist forced relocation by the U.S. government.

Don Nardo, *The Relocation of the North American Indian.* San Diego: KidHaven Press, 2002. This informative volume aimed at grade school readers tells the tragic story of the systematic dispossession of Native Americans from their lands and way of life by the relentless encroachment of white civilization in the eighteenth and nineteenth centuries.

Michael Bad Hand Terry, *Daily Life in a Plains Indian Village 1868.* Boston: Houghton Mifflin, 1999. A very colorful and lively synopsis of the way the Plains Indians lived at the time of their conquest by the United States.

Major Works Consulted

Norman Bancroft-Hunt, *Warriors: Warfare and the Native American Indian.* London: Salamander Books, 1995. An extremely well-researched synopsis of all aspects of Indian warfare and weaponry, emphasizing differences from one region and tribe to another. Highly recommended.

Dee Brown, *Bury My Heart at Wounded Knee: An Indian History of the American West.* New York: Holt, Rinehart and Winston, 1970. This powerful overview of the destruction of Indian civilization by the United States contains numerous descriptions of Native American warfare, including a moving account of the Ghost Dance and tragic incident at Wounded Knee. Highly recommended.

Paul H. Carlson, *The Plains Indians.* College Station: Texas A&M University Press, 1998. Contains much information about Indian warfare, including weapons, Indian attitudes about war, and an entire chapter on how horses transformed Plains warfare.

George Catlin, *Letters and Notes on the Manners, Customs, and Conditions of North American Indians.* 2 vols. 1844. Reprint. New York: Dover, 1973. One of the most important works ever written about Native Americans. Catlin studied numerous tribes firsthand, recording much about their cultures, including information about their weapons and fighting tactics. Highly recommended for serious students of American Indians.

Robert Hofsinde, *Indian Warriors and Their Weapons.* New York: William Morrow, 1965. A very informative discussion of Indian warfare and weapons.

Frederick E. Hoxie, ed., *Encyclopedia of North American Indians.* Boston: Houghton Mifflin, 1996. A large, highly informative overview of the tribes, leaders, experiences, and problems of Native Americans, including descriptions of warfare and weapons.

William B. Kessel, *Native American Wars and Warfare.* New York: Facts On File, 2002. An impressive work that summarizes both the reasons and the ways that the Indians fought.

Reginald Laubin, *American Indian Archery.* Norman: University of Oklahoma Press,

1991. Far and away the most comprehensive book available on the subject.

Douglas E. Leach, *Flintlock and Tomahawk: New England in King Philip's War.* New York: Macmillan, 1958. This very well-written account of a major Indian–white confrontation provides insights into the differing ways the two sides viewed the institution of war.

S.L.A. Marshall, *Crimsoned Prairie: The Wars Between the United States and the Plains Indians During the Winning of the West.* New York: Scribner's, 1972. One of the more informative and moving overviews of the wars between the United States and the Plains Indians.

Peter Nabokov, ed., *Native American Testimony.* New York: Harper and Row, 1978. One of the best existing collections of original documents pertaining to the history and struggle of the Native Americans.

Frank R. Secoy, *Changing Military Patterns of the Great Plains Indians.* Norman: University of Oklahoma Press, 1992. Traces the evolution of warfare in the plains, including discussions of prehorse, posthorse, pregun, and postgun fighting. An important book.

Edward H. Spicer, *A Short History of the Indians of the United States.* New York: D. Van Nostrand, 1969. This readable brief history contains an extensive collection of primary source documents about Native Americans.

Armstrong Starkey, *European and Native American Warfare, 1675–1815.* Norman: University of Oklahoma Press, 1998. Contains a good deal of valuable information about differing cultural aspects of Indian and white warfare, as well as descriptions of the weapons used.

Colin F. Taylor, *Native American Weapons.* Norman: University of Oklahoma Press, 2001. A fine, up-to-date, handsomely illustrated overview of the subject. Highly recommended.

John Tebbel and Keith Jennison, *The American Indian Wars.* New York: Harper and Brothers, 1960. This is a very well-researched, well-documented, and well-written synopsis of the Indian wars.

Frederick W. Turner, ed., *The Portable North American Indian Reader.* New York: Viking Press, 1974. An excellent collection of original documents about and quotes by Native Americans.

Dale Van Every, *The Disinherited: The Lost Birthright of the American Indian.* New York: Morrow, 1976. This powerful look at Indian removal and relocation, which includes numerous excerpts from primary sources, is one of the best books ever written about the Indians.

Wilcomb E. Washburn, ed., *The Indian and the White Man.* Garden City, NY: Doubleday, 1964. Contains many fascinating primary sources relating to various Native American tribes and their leaders and experiences.

Additional Works Consulted

Steve Alley and Jim Hamm, *Encyclopedia of Native American Bows, Arrows, and Quivers: Northeast, Southeast, and Midwest.* Guilford, CT: Lyons Press, 1999.

Alan Axelrod, *Chronicle of the Indian Wars, from Colonial Times to Wounded Knee.* New York: Prentice-Hall, 1993.

John Bakeless, *Eyes of Discovery.* New York: Dover, 1961.

Nancy B. Black and Bette S. Weidman, eds., *White of Red: Images of the American Indian.* Port Washington, NY: Kennikat Press, 1976.

Cyrus T. Brady, *Indian Fights and Fighters.* Lincoln: University of Nebraska Press, 1971.

Ray Brandes, ed., *Troopers West: Military and Indian Affairs on the American Frontier.* San Diego: Frontier Heritage Press, 1970.

Benjamin Capps, *The Indians.* New York: Time-Life Books, 1973.

Ward Churchill, *A Little Matter of Genocide: Holocaust Denial in the Americas, 1492 to the Present.* San Francisco: City Lights Books, 1997.

Evan S. Connell, *Son of the Morning Star: Custer and the Little Bighorn.* San Francisco: North Point Press, 1984.

Elliott Coues, ed., *The History of the Lewis and Clark Expedition.* 3 vols. New York: Francis P. Harper, 1893.

Carlton Culmsee, *Utah's Black Hawk War.* Logan: Utah State University Press, 1973.

Edward S. Curtis, *The North American Indian.* 20 vols. Cambridge, MA: Cambridge University Press, 1907–1930.

John C. Dann, ed., *The Revolution Remembered: Eyewitness Accounts of the War for Independence.* Chicago: University of Chicago Press, 1980.

Garcilaso De La Vega, *Florida of the Inca.* Trans. John and Jeannette Varner. Houston: University of Texas Press, 1951.

Gregory E. Dowd, *A Spirited Resistance: The North American Indian Struggle for Unity, 1745–1815.* Baltimore: Johns Hopkins University Press, 1992.

John Ehle, *Trail of Tears: The Rise and Fall of the Cherokee Nation.* New York: Doubleday, 1988.

Peter Farb, *Man's Rise to Civilization as Shown by the Indians of North America from Primeval Times to the Coming of the Industrial State*. New York: E.P. Dutton, 1968.

T.R. Fehrenbach, *Comanches: The Destruction of a People*. New York: Da Capo Press, 1994.

Grant Foreman, *Indian Removal*. Norman: University of Oklahoma Press, 1972.

Emma L. Fundeburk, *Southeastern Indians: Life Portraits, 1564–1860*. Metuchen, NJ: Scarecrow, 1969.

Jerome A. Greene, ed., *Battles and Skirmishes of the Great Sioux War, 1876–1877: A Military View*. Norman: University of Oklahoma Press, 1993.

James M. Hadden, *A Journal Kept in Canada and Upon Burgoyne's Campaign in 1776 and 1777*. Albany, NY: Joel Munsell's Sons, 1884.

Lawrence M. Hauptman, *The Iroquois Struggle for Survival*. Syracuse, NY: Syracuse University Press, 1986.

Ian V. Hogg, *Armies of the American Revolution*. Englewood Cliffs, NJ: Prentice-Hall, 1975.

Stanley Hoig, *The Sand Creek Massacre*. Norman: University of Oklahoma Press, 1961.

———, *Tribal Wars of the Southern Plains*. Norman: University of Oklahoma Press, 1993.

Archer Jones, *The Art of War in the Western World*. New York: Oxford University Press, 1987.

Grant Keddie, "The Atlatl Weapon," *Royal British Columbia Museum,* 1995. http://rbcm1.rbcm.gov.bc.ca.

John Keegan, *Fields of Battle: The Wars for North America*. New York: Knopf, 1996.

Stephen Longstreet, *War Cries on Horseback: The Story of the Indian Wars of the Great Plains*. New York: W.H. Allen, 1971.

Patrick M. Malone, *The Skulking Way of War: Technology and Tactics Among the New England Indians*. Baltimore: Johns Hopkins University Press, 1993.

Paula M. Marks, *In a Barren Land: American Indian Dispossession and Survival*. New York: Morrow, 1998.

Lee Miller, ed., *From the Heart: Voices of the American Indian*. New York: Random House, 1995.

James Mooney, *The Ghost Dance Religion and the Sioux Outbreak of 1890*. Lincoln: University of Nebraska Press, 1991.

J. Jay Myers, *Red Chiefs and White Challengers: Confrontations in American Indian History*. New York: Washington Square Press, 1971.

Roger C. Owens et al., eds., *The North American Indians: A Sourcebook*. New York: Macmillan, 1967.

Harold L. Peterson, *American Indian Tomahawks*. New York: Museum of the American Indian, 1971.

Zebulon Pike, *An Account of Expeditions to the Sources of the Mississippi, and Through the Western Parts of Louisiana*. Philadelphia: C. and A. Conrad, 1810.

Annette Rosenstiel, *Red and White: Indian Views of the White Man, 1492–1982*. New York: Universe Books, 1983.

Marvin C. Ross, ed., *The West of Alfred Jacob Miller.* Norman: University of Oklahoma Press, 1968.

R.F. Spencer and J. D. Jennings, *The Native Americans.* New York: Harper and Row, 1965.

Ian K. Steele, *Warpaths: Invasions of North America.* New York: Oxford University Press, 1994.

Edgar I. Stewart, *Custer's Luck.* Norman: University of Oklahoma Press, 1955.

William O. Taylor, *With Custer on the Little Bighorn.* New York: Viking, 1996.

Robert M. Utley, *The Last Days of the Sioux Nation.* New Haven, CT: Yale University Press, 1963.

Robert M. Utley and Wilcomb E. Washburn, *Indian Wars.* Boston: Houghton Mifflin, 1977.

Carl Waldman, *Atlas of the North American Indian.* New York: Facts On File, 1985.

Anthony F.C. Wallace, *The Long, Bitter Trail: Andrew Jackson and the Indians.* New York: Hill and Wang, 1993.

Paul I. Wellman, *Indian Wars and Warriors.* Boston: Houghton Mifflin, 1959.

James Wyckoff, *Famous Guns That Won the West.* New York: Arco, 1968.

Howard Zinn, *A People's History of the United States.* New York: HarperCollins, 1980.

Index

Picture Credits

About the Author

Historian and award-winning author Don Nardo has written many books for young adults about American history, including *The U.S. Presidency; The Mexican-American War; The Declaration of Independence;* biographies of Thomas Jefferson, Andrew Johnson, and Franklin D. Roosevelt; and a survey of the weapons and tactics of the American Revolution. Nardo lives with his wife, Christine, in Massachusetts.